Our AUSTRALIA DAY

CHANGING THE DATE?

JULIAN LUCAS

Published in Australia by Sid Harta Books & Print Pty Ltd,
ABN: 34632585293
23 Stirling Crescent, Glen Waverley, Victoria 3150 Australia
Telephone: +61 3 9560 9920, Facsimile: +61 3 9545 1742
E-mail: author@sidharta.com.au

First published in Australia 2025
This edition published 2025
Copyright © Julian Lucas 2025
Cover design, typesetting: WorkingType (www.workingtype.com.au)

The right of Julian Lucas to be identified as the
Author of the Work has been asserted in accordance with the
Copyright, Designs and Patents Act 1988.

All rights reserved. No part of this publication may be reproduced, stored in a retrieval system, or transmitted, in any form or by any means without the prior written permission of the publisher, nor be otherwise circulated in any form of binding or cover other than that in which it is published and without a similar condition being imposed on the subsequent purchaser.

ISBN: 978-1-922958-89-1

About the Author

The author is a retired lawyer with over fifty years' experience in practice. He is an honorary member of the Law Institute of Victoria and an honorary life member of Communications Rights Australia.

He is descended from five convicts including the wife of Thomas Lucas, Anne Howard, and members of the Abel, Thornton, and Sherburd families. He is also descended from the first qualified solicitor to come to Australia who was Thomas Hibbins, the first legal officer on Norfolk Island. His relatives in Australia, mainly somewhat distant, would number some thousands. If the two Lucas men on the First Fleet were related, then this author would also be related distantly to two other convicts from the First Fleet: Nathaniel Lucas, and Olivier Gascoigne who married and had thirteen children. If so, the number of distant relatives would increase by over 30,000. The author is also descended from families with the names Ryan, Nolan, Fern and Fisher among others.

Other books by the author

A Strategic Plan for Taxation and Welfare Reform
(Unrequited Authors Society, 2018)

Three Cases of Unrequited Justice (2019)

All About Probate: A Pocket Book Guide for Executors, ISBN 9780645269130, (2023)

Autobiographies

While I was Making Plans

Regrets Too Few to Mention

Acknowledgements

I wish to acknowledge the substantial contribution to my work by my wife Bernice and my children, in particular my daughter Louise and my oldest son Peter who have all given me a great deal of encouragement and support.

Contents

Acknowledgements — v
Preface — 1
Introduction — 3

Part One: Colonies, slavery and the First Fleet — 5
    Chapter One: Colonisation — 7
    Chapter Two: Slavery — 10
    Chapter Three: The First Fleet — 12
    Chapter Four: The marines — 20

Part Two: The superior races and our sacrifices — 23
    Chapter Five: The superior races – Germany — 25
    Chapter Six: The superior races – Japan — 28

Part Three: Aboriginal lives, violence, disease and the missionaries — 45
    Chapter Seven: The Aboriginals, their population and *terra nullius* — 47
    Chapter Eight: The lives of Aboriginals (men and women) — 54
    Chapter Nine: Aboriginal deaths from conflicts — 63
    Chapter Ten: The impact of disease — 70

Chapter Eleven: The invasion or settlement	77
Chapter Twelve: Violence towards the settlers	83
Chapter Thirteen: The missionaries	86

Part Four: The stolen generation and compensation for loss — 91

Chapter Fourteen: The stolen generation	93
Chapter Fifteen: The compensation	100

Part Five: Moral issues and other issues — 109

Chapter Sixteen: The moral issues	111
Chapter Seventeen: Current issues	115
Chapter Eighteen: The gap	130

Bibliography	137

Preface

The current federal government has given permission for eighty-one municipal councils to move away from Australia Day with their citizenship ceremonies. However, according to Wikipedia, Australia Day has become the biggest annual civic event in Australia.

Peter Dutton, Leader of the Federal Opposition and his Shadow Minister for Aboriginal Affairs, Jacinta Nampijinpa Price, wrote jointly in *The Australian* newspaper of 25 January 2024:

> Australia is not a lucky country by chance. Every Australian today is a beneficiary of what our forebears built. Living in one of the safest, most egalitarian and prosperous nations in the world, Australians have an advantage that citizens of many other countries could never imagine and could only dream of. And yet as Australia Day approaches, the usual suspects are out in force trying to feed us a diet of national self-loathing ... Most disgracefully, 81 councils have cancelled citizenship ceremonies after having been given that authority by the federal Labor government ... we need to reinvigorate our national pride ... choose resilience over victimhood, gratitude over resentment, forgiveness over retribution ... truth over falsehood ... (and push) back against those who want us to hate ourselves and our history.

This book supports these views. The author believes that there is an inadequate understanding of the significance of our national day. What Australia Day represents is a celebration of a great feat of leadership and seamanship and also the most important event in the known history of the continent of Australia. It involved a fleet of eleven small craft, each not much larger than a tennis court, carrying in all about 1500 people over 27,000 kilometres in a journey which took eight months and had a minimal loss of life with the object of creating a settlement. The date chosen for celebration was the date the flag of Great Britain was planted by the governor, Arthur Phillip, to mark the establishment of the settlement.

Australia Day was adopted in 1946 by all states, territories and the Commonwealth. Previously, it had been called Foundation Day and in Sydney 'First Landing Day'.

Some people wish to change the date of Australia Day because it celebrates the arrival of the British and the commencement of the dispossession of the land used by the Aboriginals. While there was a dispossession of the semi-nomadic native tribes, ultimately the success of the settlement was hugely beneficial to the descendants of those people, and in particular to the women who were at the time of the First Fleet permanently enslaved by their male partners throughout the continent.

This author had two ancestors on the First Fleet; neither of them were convicts. He is also descended from a number of convicts.

Introduction

This book is divided into five parts.

Part One discusses the extent of colonialism in the world at the time of the First Fleet, the significance of slavery at the time, the composition of the membership of the First Fleet and the journey itself.

In Part Two, it is sought to make the point that, in the event that Australia and its allies had been unsuccessful in the world wars, the fate of Aboriginals in the country is likely to have been persecution and probable extinction at the hands of the victors in the conflicts. It invites readers to appreciate the sacrifices made by the descendants of convicts, settlers and later immigrants in defending the country from threatened invasions.

Part Three looks at the position of Aboriginals at the time of the settlement by the members of the First Fleet, including their lifestyle, and at the impact upon them, including the effect of introduced diseases and the general dispossession which occurred. The impact of the missionaries who came to the colonies hoping to convert the natives is also discussed, as it has been suggested that without the support of the Aboriginals by the missionaries, they may well have faced extinction altogether.

Part Four concerns the story of the 'stolen generation' and the level of compensation which has been paid and is being paid for the loss caused by the dispossession and consequent devastation affecting Aboriginals.

Part Five deals with issues of moral and other concerns, the government objective of 'closing the gap', the Uluru Statement from the Heart, the Aboriginal 'flag' and possible endeavours to move towards a better future for Aboriginals still affected by traditional cultural concerns.

PART ONE
Colonies, slavery and the First Fleet

Chapter One

Colonisation

At one stage, this author considered it respectful to Aboriginal people to consider changing the date of the national day of celebration of the origins of Australia (which did not exist as a nation in any form before 1788 and in fact was not a nation until 1901), but he changed his mind. It is said that 26 January 1788 was the day Australia was 'invaded' by the British. Of course, as many do not realise, it was not the date that the First Fleet arrived, as it arrived at Botany Bay over a period of three days commencing on 18 January 1788. Perhaps 18 January could be offered up for 'Invasion Day', although the slur might be passed over in favour of another name such as 'Aboriginal Day' or as in Canada 'National Indigenous Peoples Day'. In fact, we already have numerous celebratory days for Aboriginals.

On 26 January, Governor Arthur Phillip planted a British flag at Sydney Cove which marked the establishment of the settlement as a prison colony. At the time, settlement or invasion of countries regarded as primitive societies by countries whose residents generally had superior weapons to the local groups was fairly common. It happened all over the world in large countries and continents like South, North and Central America, Africa, Indonesia and the Philippines, as well as smaller countries like

New Zealand, New Caledonia, Malaya, Hong Kong, Sri Lanka, the Canary Islands, Fiji, Brunei, Burma, Vietnam, the Polynesian islands and many other small countries and islands. In addition, there were the large-scale intrusions into India, Afghanistan and, to some extent, China.

Many of the countries which did a lot of the colonising were European and included Great Britain, France, Germany, the Netherlands, Belgium, Portugal and Spain. All of these countries had colonies in Asia or the Pacific Ocean as well as in Africa and the Americas.

Consider the following. Britain controlled Egypt and Queen Victoria became Empress of India. The French controlled the Ivory Coast which was known as Cote d'Ivoire. The Dutch controlled South Africa and the Dutch East Indies became Indonesia in due course. The French occupied Mauritius, Lebanon, Tahiti, Noumea, parts of North America and Africa and a large part of South-east Asia. The Spanish controlled the Philippines, most of the countries in South and Central America and Mexico. The Congo was occupied partly by Belgium and partly by France. Portugal occupied Brazil, Macau in China, Cochin and Goa in India and Malacca in Malaya.

Just to mention the experiences of one group affected by the Spanish intrusion, you might consider the Incas and their last king, Atahualpa. He was captured by the Spanish after their relatively small group of 168 men killed 2000 of the Incas in one confrontation. He then tried to bribe his capturers, headed by Francisco Pizarro, by giving them a roomful of gold. He filled the room to the extent that, apart from Fort Knox, there would rarely, if ever, have been such a quantity of gold in one building. They gave him the choice of a painful death by fire or, if he agreed to convert to Christianity, they would simply kill him by garrotting, to which he duly agreed to succumb.

Chapter Two

Slavery

When the First Fleet was travelling to Australia, it had three stops on the way: the Canary Islands, Rio de Janeiro and Cape Town, all places which had been colonised and held respectively by Spain, Portugal and the Netherlands. Happily for Captain Phillip, and unusually, Britain was not at war with any of these countries at the time.

One characteristic of these other countries was that, at that time, they all practised slavery. Rio had a large population of African slaves. WikiAnswers states that about two million Africans died in the course of transportation to the Americas as slaves. Other sources suggest the figures may be a great deal higher. Many of the slaves were not initially sent to the United States but many were transferred there later from other places. To gain an idea of the size of the extent of slavery, consider that when the American Civil War ended, Wikipedia reports that there were about three million slaves freed in the American colonies.

You will probably know that Captain Phillip famously announced that there would be no slavery in a colony which he governed. Even after he had nearly been killed by a spear-throwing Aboriginal, Phillip did not seek any reprisal. Of course, he did later carry out a reprisal raid after the Aboriginals had killed about seventeen of the settlers, but that was not part of a pattern of violent conduct towards Aboriginals in general.

It is clear that the major proponent for the cessation of slavery throughout the world was Great Britain. The suppression of slavery by the British was carried out at considerable cost to Britain.

If Australia had been colonised by one of the other European powers, it is fair to say that the probability of enslaving parts of the Aboriginal population would have been quite high. In addition, if, for example, the Spanish had brought to Australia their attitude towards indigenous people which they exercised in South America, one can hardly expect that the Aboriginals would have received the same courtesies offered by Governor Phillip.

North of Australia in Makassar, the Dutch had in earlier times taken natives and sold them as slaves as reported by Spanish visitors and noted in the book, *1787*, by Nick Brodie.

Professor James Allan in an article in *Spectator* magazine of June 2024 wrote as follows:

> ... a majority cohort of our young ... believe their countries have uniquely bad histories rather than ones that have created the best places to live – especially for women and minorities – in the history of the world and in the case of Britain it was the only country that spent huge amounts of its own monies to end slavery, an institution that existed everywhere on earth with no other places or cultures making big sacrifices or doing anything at all to end it.

Chapter Three

The First Fleet

The First Fleet left Portsmouth Harbour on Sunday, 13 May 1787. It has inspired quite a few books. It appears that a lot of the assertions and assumptions about the Fleet in various books have been incorrect. Emeritus Professor Alan Frost, in one of several books he has written, (*The First Fleet: The Real Story*, published in 2012), and to which this author will refer as a reliable source, has clearly examined a huge amount of primary material, in particular for the purpose of correcting some of the earlier erroneous statements concerning the Fleet.

Professor Frost tells us that the number of people who embarked on the First Fleet was not less than 1420 and taking into account births and deaths during the voyage, the number who arrived in New South Wales was 1373. There were 759 convicts, comprising 568 men and 191 women. A small number of convicts who had been committed for the voyage died before the departure, and two who had been committed to the voyage avoided it by receiving pardons just in time. The number of marines was 332, of whom the majority were volunteers. In addition, as private marines, they were permitted to take wives; there were twenty-eight of these and twenty-four children. Among the marines was the ancestor of this author, Thomas

Lucas, the grandfather of this author's great-grandfather. (The marines are discussed in the next chapter.)

There remains uncertainty about the number of crews members on the ships. Professor Frost believes that there were approximately 210 in the crews of the six convict transport ships and the three storeships. One reason why there remains uncertainty is that these nine ships were not government vessels but were privately contracted for the voyage. Professor Frost thinks there were probably quite a few more than this and could have been as many as 100 extra crewmen. The fixed complement of the government ships, the *Sirius* and the *Supply*, were stated to be 160 and 55 respectively.

The major contractor for supplying the voyage was William Richards Jr and it is fair to say that he received compliments on his performance. One omission which this author observed in Professor Frost's account is a person of importance to this author. This was the presence among the passengers of one Zachariah Clarke who was the agent of the contractor and was probably the first person in Australia to operate something resembling a shop. Zachariah was a direct ancestor of this author, being the grandfather of this author's great-grandmother.

Professor Frost lists a number of conclusions from his research, including the following:

1. There was no selection of convict women, by age or other criteria.
2. There was no selection of convict men by age.
3. There may have been some selection of male convicts according to skill. The convict, Nathaniel Lucas, was

a carpenter and was responsible for construction of a number of buildings in the colony, both in Norfolk Island and in Sydney. The relationship between the two Lucas men on the fleet is uncertain, although they were both from the same town in Surrey.
4. There was some selection of personnel other than convicts according to skills that might prove useful. This author's ancestor, Thomas Lucas, was a glazier as well as a marine.
5. The average age of the convicts was about twenty-seven. Most of them had been sentenced to seven years of transportation.

Arthur Phillip proved to be a very good choice to lead the voyage and to establish the colony. He was intelligent and resourceful and he put considerable effort into the preparation of the First Fleet. He spoke five languages; namely, French, German, Portuguese, Spanish and, of course, his own. He had been a spy for the British government in France for some time, during which he may have observed the preparations for the voyage of the French which was planned to visit the Pacific Ocean under their leader, La Perouse. After the First Fleet arrived, it had almost immediate contact with the French voyagers when the two French ships appeared outside Botany Bay. The French ships stayed at Botany Bay for a short period and had some friendly contacts with the British.

Phillip had also been made available to the Portuguese navy for about four years to command ships among other things being used to transfer convicts to South America.

The first part of the voyage of the First Fleet was to reach the

Canary Islands held by the Spanish. The Canary Islands are near the Tropic of Cancer and have a sub-tropical climate. As the Fleet proceeded into the tropics, various creatures emerged from the woodwork on the ships, including rats, mice, mosquitoes and spiders.

The Fleet spent one week at Santa Cruz, the chief town on the island of Tenerife. The convicts were reported as generally behaving well. There was a small insurrection which was dealt with appropriately, and the Fleet proceeded to Rio de Janeiro in Brazil.

During this part of the voyage, the Fleet passed over the equator and the traditional tribute to King Neptune was performed. A small craft was encountered which had been to the Falkland Islands and it was learnt that the vessel had been crossing and re-crossing the equator a number of times because of the lack of suitable wind. This lack of wind caused the area around the equator to be described as the doldrums. These ships had nothing like the clever rudders used later that would have reduced the impact of poor winds.

The Fleet reached Rio de Janeiro, which was under the control of the Portuguese who greeted Phillip warmly, reflecting his previous service to the Portuguese. Rio is very close to the Tropic of Capricorn which is the tropic which runs through Australia at Rockhampton in Queensland. This gives an indication of how little of Australia is in the tropics.

After about a month in Rio, the Fleet moved forward on 4 September and arrived in Cape Town on 13 October. After purchasing stores, the Fleet left Cape Town on 11 November for the longest part of the voyage. It seems that the Fleet was then blown off course quite a distance by unfavourable winds before heading east.

Tasmania, previously known as Van Diemen's Land, was sighted on 6 January 1788. Professor Frost quotes from David Collins who was appointed as Deputy Judge-Advocate (although not a lawyer, he was the first legal officer in the colony):

> Thus, under the blessing of God, was happily completed, in eight months and one week, a voyage which, before it was undertaken, the mind hardly dared venture to contemplate ... we had sailed 5021 leagues [27,894 kilometres] ... without meeting any accident in a fleet of eleven sail, nine of which were merchantmen that had never sailed in that distant and imperfectly explored ocean ... [of the convicts] only thirty-two had died since their leaving England, among whom were to be included one or two deaths by accident ...

David Collins also wrote:

> ... the high health which was apparent in every countenance was to be attributed not only to the refreshments we met with at Rio de Janeiro and the Cape of Good Hope but to the excellent quality of the provisions with which we were supplied by Mr. Richards Jr. the contractor.

In a letter to the editor of *The Australian* on 26 January 2022, Peter Waterhouse states that the First Fleet was 'disease ridden'. Not so according to two who were there. Philip Gidley King wrote in his journal after arriving in Cape Town:

> the whole number of sick [on the First Fleet] did not exceed 20 and those few were re-established in 3 or 4 days after

arrival & continued so till the day of our departure, nor did we land either soldier or sailor at Sick Quarters which is a very rare circumstance at this place.

The figures are sometimes conflicted but it appears that there were forty-eight deaths during the voyage and twenty-eight live births. Given the class of people who were convicts, such numbers of deaths may well have occurred if they had stayed at home. (The Second Fleet was an entirely different story.)

While Phillip is said to have planted a flag on 26 January 1788, marking his arrival at Sydney Cove, the official date of establishment of the colony was 7 February. Having discovered that Botany Bay was not particularly suitable for a settlement because there was inadequate running water, and after exploring Port Jackson, Sydney Cove within that port was chosen as the site for the settlement. On 7 February, after unloading most of the stores and all of the convicts, the colonists were assembled on the west side of the cove with the marines entering by marching with their band. Phillip stood bareheaded in company with his principal officers. David Collins read Phillip's commission and letters patent establishing the colony's courts. The band played 'God Save the King' and the marines fired volleys.

Irish convicts

Between 1787 and 1868, the number of convicts sent to Australia was about 162,000 of which 39,000 were Irish from Ireland. The First Fleet had a small number of Irish from England as well as some French, some Americans and some black men. Since Ireland was being occupied by the British, it may be argued that those who were transported were political prisoners. (Some were actually classified as such.) There was a rebellion in Ireland in 1798 which was crushed. Irish men were sent to Australia as convicts and some of them could not speak English, being from those parts of Ireland described as the Gaeltacht in which the Irish language is spoken.

At the time of the First Fleet, it was illegal in Britain to practise the Catholic religion. Legislation to reverse that position was introduced in 1791, and later the Catholic Emancipation Act of 1829 gave Catholics most normal legal rights (although the British monarch still cannot be a Catholic).

Among later Irish convicts was a famous Irishman named John Mitchel. He had been a lawyer and later a journalist. He was not a Catholic, which alone made his position unusual. In 1848, the third year of the potato famine in Ireland, he attacked the British verbally and constantly. He maintained that the settled policy of England was to reduce the population of Ireland to easy governable limits. Mitchel wrote as follows:

> The English Government never yet observed any single treaty which it was convenient for them to break … having solemnly agreed by the capitulation of Limerick NOT to impose penalties for Catholic worship, and having so disarmed the Catholic forces and ended the war, that Government, as a matter of course, at once imposed penal laws (seriously restricting Catholics) …

Mitchel quotes the famous Anglo-Irish philosopher, Edmund

Burke, as calling the penal code 'a machine of wise and deliberate contrivance as well fitted for the oppression, impoverishment and degradation of a people, and the debasement in them of human nature itself, as ever proceeded from the perverted ingenuity of man'.

The Irish people were, as Mitchel claimed, 'impoverished and debased'. He quoted Bishop Berkeley, a famous Irish philosopher, who had asked in 1734 'whether there be on earth any Christian or civilised people so beggarly, wretched and destitute as the common Irish?'

The population of Ireland in 1841 was around 8.2 million. In 1861, it was 6.5 million.

After a political trial, Mitchel was imprisoned in Bermuda before being taken to Van Diemen's Land. Mitchel escaped and went to New York where he founded an expatriate newspaper called *The Citizen*.

It is possible that about twenty-five to thirty per cent of Australians have some Irish heritage.

Chapter Four

The marines

Thomas Lucas, the ancestor of this author, was a marine. Marines were classified as being soldiers capable of being able to fight at sea. No doubt the marines were chosen instead of members of the regular army because of the long sea voyage, and that they would have thought to have been less likely to have been affected by seasickness.

Joseph Matra, an American, was an important and well-regarded contributor to the proposal to establish a colony in New South Wales. He had been a midshipman under Captain Cook on the *Endeavour* when it had entered Botany Bay. Matra made a submission to government about the proposed colony, though he had no official position at the time. Initially, he thought the colony should be established with poor people to take them away from criminal conduct in England and with some of those who had left America after the War of Independence. He changed his mind and accepted the proposal to people the new colony with convicts.

There were three locations on the English coast which provided bases for the marines, and the marines for the First Fleet were initially chosen from the bases at Portsmouth and Plymouth. They comprised four companies each of fifty-two men plus four others with official positions. Almost all the marines chosen for the First Fleet were volunteers. There were in fact more marines volunteering than could be chosen.

According to Professor Frost, the number of marines was initially 212 but two additional companies each of sixty men were added so that the total force was 332 men. Officers were not permitted to bring wives, but other marines were permitted to do so and as a result, twenty-eight wives and twenty-four children were able to join the fleet.

One noteworthy feature was the willingness of the marines to accept the same rations as the convicts when the colony was going through an extensive period of deprivation due to the lack of supply and crop failure. Even so, Professor Frost does not appear to have a high opinion of the marines who were part of the First Fleet. Other writers speak with more favour and compare their performance with the rather less than satisfactory behaviour of the members of the New South Wales Corps which replaced them.

This writer's ancestor, Thomas Lucas, was a Freemason. Before he left England, he handed to a friend enough money to pay for his next annual subscription to his local lodge. However, he never returned to England but became the first white person to settle at Brown's River, later called Kingston, which is near the coast just west of Hobart. This occurred after the decision was taken to abandon the first settlement on Norfolk Island. Thomas was a sergeant before he retired from the military on Norfolk. He also had a trade as a glazier.

When Thomas came to Australia, he brought with him his Masonic apron, which it seems he had received from his father.

It is kept in the Masonic Centre in Hobart in a glass case and is available to be seen by visitors. It may be the oldest piece of manufactured cloth in the country.

This author's family is proud to be celebrating Australia Day on 26 January, the date the flag was raised. Naturally, the author's family is proud of the direct connection with members of the First Fleet and the contribution they made to the settlement. As mentioned previously, Thomas was the grandfather of the great-grandfather of this author.

The other family connection, already mentioned, is with Zachariah Clark who was also on Norfolk and died there. He was the grandfather of Julia Abel, a great-grandmother of this author.

The leader of the marines was Major Ralph Ross who had a poor relationship with Governor Phillip.

John Moore, the author of *The First Fleet Marines*, had this to say:

> The general quality of the marine who came to New South Wales was, from his behaviour in the colony, superior to his counterpart in many parts of the Army. Thus, there were no murders committed by marines, they attended church parades without demur and showed a respect for religion which … was later found wanting in their successors and by their general demeanour, they made for a cohesiveness of society rather than the divisiveness created by their successors.

Part Two
The superior races and our sacrifices

Chapter Five

The superior races – Germany

It is of interest to reflect upon the possible impacts upon the Aboriginal population if either of the two world wars had been lost by the Allies.

You may recall a lesson from history of the not-too-distant past. Apart from the enormous number of deaths in the conflicts during World War II, the supposedly civilised and Christian Germans murdered 6 million people, mainly Jews, before the middle of the last century. Their justification was that their victims were of an inferior race as they were not Aryans. Mind you, Hitler was prepared to accept the English as being Aryans. Black people were clearly not Aryans in the mind of Hitler and his philosophical antecedents.

Bear in mind that in 1918, the Germans had come close to winning the Great War, particularly after the capitulation of Russia which allowed a very large number of troops to transfer from the Russian front to the conflicts in France with the Allies. The Germans had bases in the Pacific in Samoa, New Guinea and the Marshall Islands. Australians lost 62,000 of their best and bravest in the Great War plus many, many thousands more who frequently died shortly afterwards or were permanently damaged by their experiences in the conflict, including four of this writer's uncles and three of his wife's uncles. If the war had been lost by the Allies, it is reasonable to think that Australia may well have become a casualty of the peace and a German colony – what would have prevented it? As has been pointed out, if Britain had lost the war, then Germany would have taken the main mineral supplying countries of the British Empire, being Australia and Canada. This was expressed by their main military leader, General Ludendorff, who planned 'Germanisation' in conquered areas, which included Australia. (See Perry, *Monash and Chauvel*.)

During the battle for France during World War II, many soldiers from the French colonies were captured by the German forces. Most of these troops came from the French North African possessions, while around twenty per cent were from French West Africa. Influenced by Nazi racial ideology, German troops summarily killed between 1000 and 1500 black prisoners in May and June 1940. Most of the white French soldiers who surrendered were not murdered by the Germans.

Photographs of the moments just before one massacre, recently uncovered by a private collector, show the German soldiers totally calm and relaxed as they prepared to murder their approximately fifty victims (of the hundred Senegalese killed after surrendering in the area over two days). German officers specifically ordered French civilians living nearby not to bury the murdered soldiers, but instead to let them rot in the open. However, the civilians, who also sheltered a handful of Senegalese who had managed to escape, buried the bodies in a mass grave overnight.

Chapter Five The superior races – Germany

A recent BBC documentary film with Sir Tony Robinson as narrator recalled the story of the Battle of Bastogne in December 1944. The following is an account:

> An act of heroic self-sacrifice highlighted the dedicated service of the 333rd Field Artillery Battalion, a segregated African American unit that bolstered American forces in Western Europe during World War II. That sacrifice unfortunately ended in tragedy for eleven American soldiers, murdered in one of the many atrocities committed by German *Waffen-SS* troops, in this case with particular savagery because the victims were black. Compounding the tragedy, this atrocity was not officially recognized in the United States until many decades after the war had ended.

In fact, the tortures conducted by the Germans on the black soldiers in 1944 were extraordinarily barbarous and evil. The details are so horrific that they have been omitted from this account.

The American blacks were in commands segregated from the white soldiers. This arrangement persisted until as late as 1948 when it was discontinued by President Truman. (Another source has suggested that President Roosevelt had made the change before he died late in the war).

Chapter Six

The superior races – Japan

Another group with whom Hitler felt able to collaborate were the Japanese who also believed that their race was superior to that of others. On 27 September 1940, Germany, Italy and Japan signed the Tripartite Pact. This pact formalised the alliance between the three countries, subsequently referred to as the Axis powers.

Revisionist historians have suggested that the Japanese never intended to conquer Australia. This view cannot be supported by the evidence and the reality of Japanese ambitions. On the occasion of the fall of Singapore on 15 February 1942, Japan's Prime Minister, General Hideki Tojo, called on Australia to surrender to Japan. General Tojo suggested that Japan would be merciful to Australia if that happened. Tojo would repeat this demand for Australia's surrender in the Japanese parliament on 28 May 1942. To distract attention from the impending Japanese attack on America's Midway Atoll in the central Pacific, and perhaps to demonstrate Australia's vulnerability, Japanese midget submarines penetrated Sydney Harbour on 31 May 1942 and torpedoed the Royal Australian depot ship *Kattabul*, killing twenty-one sailors in Australia. One Japanese force to land in Australia during World War II was a reconnaissance party that landed in the Kimberley region of Western Australia on 19 January 1944 to investigate reports that the Allies were building large bases in the region.

Tojo's demands for surrender fell on deaf ears. The treacherous Japanese sneak attack on the American Pacific Fleet at anchor in Pearl Harbour while Japanese diplomats were still discussing peace in Washington was unlikely to produce trust by Australia in Japanese assurances.

It is inconceivable that Japan's Greater East Asia Co-Prosperity Sphere which included Australia and New Zealand would have permitted the existence of a substantial British base in the Pacific arena. It would be simplistic to think so.

In the opinion of this writer, the Battle of Midway in June 1942 may have been the most important battle of World War II for Australia and perhaps the most important battle ever for Australia. If the Battle of Midway had been lost by the Allies, the Americans might have been amenable to a peace treaty with the Japanese to avoid the Japanese attacking Hawaii (and perhaps the American West Coast) which, had they won the Battle of Midway, the Japanese would surely have wished to do.

Australia was already named as a target by the Japanese, so it is fairly obvious that Japan would have demanded that Australia be sacrificed in any peace settlement. In hindsight, it seems clear that the Japanese appreciated that they would never defeat America, but they may well have created sufficient impetus to induce the Americans to agree to a peace treaty. The Americans did not come to Australia to save Australia but to save America. It is worthy of note that there have always been many

Americans who could be described as isolationists. Before Pearl Harbour many Americans were against their country engaging in European conflicts.

The details about the Battle of Midway are interesting. It occurred after the Battle of the Coral Sea which proved to be inconclusive. Douglas MacArthur fled the Philippines and went to Australia as he had been instructed to do by President Roosevelt, and he insisted that all his army's code breakers leave and go to Australia as well. On his way across Australia travelling by train, MacArthur stopped in Adelaide long enough to make his famous speech announcing that he would return to the Philippines. On the arrival of his train in Melbourne, he was warmly greeted by a large crowd of people.

The code breakers set up three bases in Melbourne suburbs. Australia also provided men for code breaking and had them trained. It was an American code breaker in Australia who came up with the clever idea of using a message about a fictitious failure of the water purification plant on Midway Island to enable the Allies to determine from decoding Japanese messages that this was the place which the Japanese Fleet was preparing to invade. The Japanese on their part did not know that the American carriers were close by. The Japanese losses were enormous; they lost four aircraft carriers, about 300 aircraft and about 3000 men. Instead of being able to occupy some American soil in Hawaii, the Japanese were forced to retreat.

James Bowen is convener of the Battle for Australia Association. He has been an army officer, a senior Crown Prosecutor and senior public servant. He has this to say:

Chapter Six The superior races – Japan

This historical misunderstanding with regard to Japan's hostile planning for Australia in 1942 appears to have been generated between 2002 and 2006 by the Australian War Memorial's former senior historian Dr Peter Stanley, who claimed in published essays that Australia did not face a grave threat from Japan in 1942 and that Prime Minister John Curtin exaggerated the Japanese threat to Australia for political advantage.

When challenged by me to produce credible historical evidence to support these claims, Dr. Stanley was unable to do so. When invited by me to debate publicly his claims Dr. Stanley declined the offer. Dr. Stanley's controversial revisionism appeared to rely on nothing stronger than his argument that the really significant battles that decided World War II were fought in Europe.

Now that the Australian government has formally adopted commemoration of the Battle for Australia, young Australians need to appreciate that Australia faced grave peril from Japan in 1942. Control of access to Australia was considered vital by both the Japanese and Americans in 1942, and both were determined to prevent the enemy gaining that access.

To deny the Americans access to Australia for a counter-offensive, the Japanese navy general staff was proposing as early as December 1941 a limited invasion and occupation of Australia in the north. However, the Japanese army opposed an invasion of the Australian mainland on the grounds of massive troop requirement and logistical burden. In their minds, Australia could wait.

The Japanese generals, including Prime Minister General Hideki Tojo, pressed for adoption of an equally sinister plan to bring Australia to heel, called Operation FS. This plan involved isolating Australia from the United States by means of a chain of fortified Japanese-occupied islands stretching across the Pacific and subjecting Australia to intensified blockade, bombardment and psychological warfare. The generals believed that implementation of Operation FS would likely produce Australia's submission to Japan and withdrawal from the Allied cause without the need for an invasion by 'force of arms'. By 7 March 1942, the Japanese navy and army had agreed that severing Australia's lifeline to the United States (by Operation FS) and pressuring Australia into submission to Japan were more important objectives than the limited invasion of Australia's northern coast.

On 15 March 1942, with Emperor Hirohito's approval, Japan's military high command formally resolved to implement Operation FS. The Battle of the Coral Sea frustrated Japan's first attempt to implement Operation FS. The Japanese naval defeat at the Battle of Midway forced Japan to cancel the original Operation FS in July 1942 and to pursue its hostile plans for Australia by less ambitious measures such as the campaigns for Kokoda and Guadalcanal.

This account of the gravity of the Japanese threat facing Australia in 1942 is supported by the leading historians and Japan scholars, Professors Henry Frei and John J. Stephan, and by the massive official Japanese history of the Pacific war, *Senshi Sōsho*.

The number of deaths of Australian soldiers, sailors and

Chapter Six The superior races – Japan

airmen killed in the New Guinea conflict – either in action, dying from wounds or captured and killed while prisoners of the Japanese – is uncertain. Some of those captured were taken by the Japanese to Burma and many of those died there. James P. Duffy, the American author of *War at the End of the World* wrote that there were 7000 Australian deaths during the conflict and a similar number of Americans. Australian Phillip Bradley, author of *Hell's Battlefield*, lists in detail the numbers killed from each army unit, and the total of his list is about 8000 Australians.

How important was the New Guinea campaign to the Japanese? James Duffy in *War at the End of the World* states that the Japanese lost over 200,000. Another account puts their losses at 202,100 in various islands in or near New Guinea. They also lost soldiers in ships coming to New Guinea and its near neighbours as a result of air strikes by the Allies.

If the Japanese had had their wish and Australia had surrendered, how would they have behaved? With decency, respect, fairness, understanding, compassion, honesty and consideration for the original native inhabitants? Let us consider some examples of their conduct.

1. As part of the evacuation of wounded service personnel and nurses from Singapore just before it fell to the Japanese, the Sarawak royal yacht, SS *Vyner Brooke*, carried away nurses, wounded personnel and civilian men, women and children. It was sunk by the Japanese and the ship's lifeboats took most of the people to islands, including about 100 survivors who reunited on Bangka Island near Muntok, a town in the Dutch East Indies, now

Indonesia, occupied by the Japanese. Included with these were twenty-two nurses. When they learned that the island was held by the Japanese, an officer from the ship went to Muntok to surrender. The civilian women and children also left for Muntok.

The nurses stayed to care for the wounded and set up a shelter with a large Red Cross sign on it. The ship's officer returned with about twenty Japanese soldiers. All of the wounded who could walk were taken around a headland and the nurses heard shots, after which the Japanese soldiers returned without the wounded men and cleaned their weapons.

A Japanese officer ordered the twenty-two nurses and one civilian woman to walk into the water. When they were waist-deep, a machine gun set up on the beach opened fire and murdered all of them except one, the famous Lieutenant-Colonel Sister Vivian Bullwinkel who was shot in the stomach and pretended to be dead. The Japanese then murdered the remaining wounded and helpless prisoners by bayonetting them to death.

After lying unconscious for some time, Sister Bullwinkel managed to get away and surrendered to other Japanese who placed her in a camp where she stayed for three years, never daring to mention her experience until she was able to give evidence at a war crimes trial in Tokyo in 1947. It now seems quite likely that the nurses were raped by the Japanese before they were murdered. It is believed that Sister Bullwinkel was asked not to mention the rapes out of regard for the feelings of the relatives of those murdered.

2. In another case of a POW massacre, the Japanese stationed in Palawan Island in the Philippines tried to kill all their American prisoners after wrongly assuming Allied forces had invaded. After driving the prisoners into makeshift air raid shelters, the Japanese burned them alive. Those who fled the burning structures were bayonetted, shot or bludgeoned to death. A few dozen managed to make it as far as the shoreline and hide there; the Japanese caught, tortured and executed almost all of them. Of the 150 prisoners, less than a dozen survived to tell the tale, the lucky few somehow finding the strength to swim across a bay to safety.

3. Even the small South Pacific island of Nauru did not escape the horrors of the war. After a raid on the island's airfield by American bombers in March 1943, the Japanese beheaded and bayoneted five interned Australians in retaliation. That same year, the Japanese also forcibly deported more than 1000 indigenous inhabitants as labour to other occupied islands to conserve rations. During their occupation, the Japanese exterminated the island's leper colony. Stowing the island's thirty-nine lepers on a boat, the Japanese led them far out to sea and out of sight. Japanese gun boats then fired at the vessel, sinking it and killing all on board.

4. The Japanese destroyer, *Akikaze*, voyaging to the Japanese stronghold in Rabaul in New Britain, picked up German

missionaries and Chinese civilians living in the South Pacific islands of Kairiru and Manus. En route to their destination, the captain of the ship received instructions to execute the entire group. To accomplish this quietly, the Japanese led their victims one by one to the back of the ship to a makeshift gallows.

After securing the victims' wrists to a pulley, the Japanese whipped and shot them, then sent their bodies overboard. The sounds of the ship and the wind prevented victims from suspecting anything until the last moment. After three hours, the Japanese had successfully killed all sixty passengers, including a child approaching five years of age whom they threw overboard while still alive.

5. Following the fall of Singapore, the Japanese wanted to mop up all remaining resistance, especially among Chinese living in the region. To accomplish this, the notorious Japanese secret police, the Kempeitai, initiated Operation Sook Ching ('purging through cleansing') in February 1942.

Singapore was the first to be purged. After interning and interrogating the city's entire Chinese population, the Kempeitai herded those they deemed as dangerous into military vehicles. They then transported them to the city's outskirts and executed them all. This purging operation soon found its way into other parts of Malaya as well. It is reported that over one million people in Malaysa were murdered. That stands alongside the 6 million or more Chinese murdered by the invading Japanese.

Chapter Six The superior races – Japan

The manpower shortage and pressure of time made the Kempeitai especially merciless towards those in rural areas. They eliminated entire villages on the mere suspicion of subversive activity.

Although we have no official casualty figures, estimates of Kempeitai-ordered deaths in Singapore range from 5000 to 6000 (Japanese sources) to a high of 30,000 to 100,000 (Singaporean and Chinese sources).

6. One of Japan's most notorious submarines, the *I-8*, is best remembered for sinking two Allied ships and for the crew's conduct in the aftermath.

On 26 March 1944, the sub spotted and sank the Dutch freighter, SS *Tjisalak*, hundreds of miles off the coast of Colombo, Sri Lanka. The Japanese took 103 survivors onboard and massacred most of them with swords and sledgehammers. They then bound those still alive and left them on deck as the submarine dived below. Only five survived.

A few months later, the Japanese destroyed the US cargo ship, SS *Jean Nicolet*, and subjected survivors to the same brutal treatment. The Japanese tortured and killed their prisoners by making them pass through a gauntlet of swords and bayonets before throwing their bodies overboard. The Japanese dived after spotting an Allied aircraft, with thirty prisoners still above deck. Only two dozen of the hundred-plus prisoners survived.

7. Early in 1945, General Yamashita planned for his men to evacuate Manila and fight in the countryside. However,

two Japanese admirals ignored his order and committed their men to a final stand inside the city. When the Americans arrived, the Japanese forces vented their rage on the hapless civilians trapped inside their lines.

For weeks, the Japanese raped, pillaged and murdered. Aside from the bayonets and beheadings, they machine-gunned captives and set fire to buildings with people trapped inside. The Americans ceased artillery strikes so the Japanese could surrender, but the Japanese instead continued their rampage.

After the dust settled, all Japanese defenders of the city had died, taking with them 100,000 civilian casualties. The incident left Manila as one of the Allies' most damaged capital cities, second only to Warsaw.

8. In the Dutch East Indies, now Indonesia, the Japanese murdered 2000 Dutch nationals in the most brutal and barbarous manner.

It is well known that frequently the Japanese ate the bodies of some of the prisoners of war after they had murdered them.

After the end of the war, a number of war crimes tribunals were created. In a well-researched book titled *Traitors* by Frank Walker, the numbers prosecuted for war crimes are listed. A number of Japanese faced the Australian military courts. The courts convicted 644 Japanese in Rabaul, Labuan, Morotai, Manus Island, Hong Kong, Singapore, Wewak and Darwin. Of these, 214 were sentenced to death of which only 137 were executed. The others received lengthy prison sentences which were generally never fully served. A total of 4488 Japanese faced trial in Allied military courts of which 1041 were given the death penalty. American military courts convicted 1229 and sentenced 163 to death. Britain convicted 811 and sentenced 265 to death. Holland convicted 969 and sentenced 236 to death. China convicted 504 and sentenced 149 to death. France convicted 198 and sentenced 63 to death. The Philippines convicted 133 and sentenced 17 to death. Soviet convictions are in general not available.

A controversy arose about the plans to prosecute the Japanese emperor. Australia's Dr Evatt (who, you may recall, was president of the United Nations General Assembly) was convinced that the emperor should be charged but the view prevailed that it was in the interests of future governing of Japan that he be allowed to live.

An important paper written by Lieutenant Charles R. Viale in May 1988 in the School of Advanced Military Studies at United States Army Command Fort Leavenworth, in Kansas, titled 'Prelude to War. Japan's Goals and Strategies in World', provides some relevant points about Japanese strategies when entering the war and the potential impact of its planning. His paper includes the following:

> Continuous propaganda had instilled a commitment to austerity and sacrifice in the name of something called the Great East Asia Co-Prosperity Sphere. This self-imposed mission, despite the murder, rape and pillage it entailed, was somehow to becomes Japan's contribution to the maintenance of peace in the world. After the war, when the former Japanese Minister of War, Hideki Tojo was questioned

about Japan's motives, he replied that "she was not seeking to exploit others or to fill her own coffers. That was absolutely not the spirit of the Great East Asia new order at all ... (It) was based on mutual benefit ...The idea was initiative and guidance, not subjugation and subordination ..."

(All) Japanese looked at Japan's position in China ([invasion by Japan] as sanctioned by economic need and by their destiny to create a new order in Asia that would expel Western influence and establish a structure based upon Asian concepts of justice and humanity ...

... Anticipated for inclusion in the Greater East Asia Co-Prosperity Sphere were China, Hong Kong, Burma, French Indo-China, Thailand, Malaya, New Guinea, India, Australia, New Zealand, the Philippines, and the Netherlands Indies ...

The Navy Chief of Staff said: "We will not thereby be able to bring the war to a conclusion ... Our Empire does not have the means to take the offensive, overcome the enemy, and make them give up their will to fight ..."

The idea of an East Asia Co-Prosperity Sphere was heralded as the ultimate Japanese purpose. It was to be a sacred war led by a sacred emperor ... (seeking) the happiness of Asian peoples ... Her Greater East Asia Co-Prosperity Sphere was the vehicle by which Japan would become the leader of the region ...

With Britain's inevitable capitulation, threats to US interests in the Western Hemisphere, and the strength of the Japanese position in the Pacific, the United States was

Chapter Six The superior races – Japan

expected to see the futility of fighting and accept Japanese terms for peace. For added assurance, propaganda would be used to appeal to antiwar sentiments in America ...

After initial operations, the Navy planned to intercept United States naval forces with a strong Pacific fleet and to occupy or destroy New Guinea, New Britain, Samoa, the Fiji Islands, the Aleutians, and parts of Australia ...

The Japanese recognized the danger of war with the United States, but they hoped to execute their plans violently and quickly, secure their objectives, and set up a defence in such depth and of such strength a settlement to the long and costly war would be required to reduce these defences ...

Professor Blainey has written:

If we had lost the war we would have been governed by a totalitarian regime. Canberra eventually would have had a puppet cabinet of Australians or a powerful Japanese governor ruling perhaps from Yarralumla. Many Australians, looking back, still suggest that it pays to lose a war. But the evidence suggests that it pays, even more, to win a war.

Readers may be aware that, unlike the situation in Germany, the Japanese do not teach their children any of this historical material. The reader is asked to reflect upon the fate of Aboriginal natives if Germany had won the Great War or the Axis powers had won World War II.

One writer expresses the sentiment of observers that the Japanese were one of the most racist societies in history, right up there and possibly worse than Nazi Germany. They believed that their superiority gave them the right to treat their inferiors any way they wanted, which left perhaps more than ten million civilian bodies in their wake.

At the end of World War II, there were about 600,000 men and women in uniform in the armed forces in Australia. In all in a total population of about 7 million, about 1 million served in uniform during the war. In addition, there had been 77,500 men conscripted for duties in Australia under the so-called 'manpower' laws. The body in charge was known as the Civil Construction Corps. Of these, 54,000 were still involved at the end of the war. These men included this author's father, a carpenter, who was a foreman to a group building aerodromes and other structures in Queensland and New South Wales. He had been away from his home in Melbourne for three years.

Additional people were involved in large numbers in manufacturing. You may recall that we manufactured aeroplanes as well as weapons such as the Owen gun, which was the only sub-machine gun designed and produced in Australia. About 45,000 Owen guns were used. The factories involved in war manufacturing included a small Melbourne factory manufacturing weapons and ammunition which survived the war and became a subject for investment by this author in 1980. That factory survives to this day.

We met the threats by foreign powers to our sovereignty with great sacrifice by our men and women, and these sacrifices made an important contribution to the success of the Allies in those conflicts. What our people did was to contribute in a fundamental way towards the prevention of the occupation of

Australia by brutal murderous powers and in particular powers that, given their previous behaviour, would not have had any particular reason to hold our Aboriginal population in high regard.

We have sacrificed over 100,000 young lives in conflicts which have been effective in keeping Australia safe for all Australians, including in particular Aboriginals who may well have faced persecution from nations whose racist tendencies were so conspicuous. In addition to the deaths in the wars, there were of course many more thousands who returned injured and impaired and who often died soon afterwards.

Part Three
Aboriginal lives, violence, disease and the missionaries

Chapter Seven

The Aboriginals, their population and *terra nullius*

It is uncertain among scholars as to how many Aboriginals were in Australia when the British arrived. Professor Geoffrey Blainey in his seminal book, *The Triumph of the Nomads*, suggest that 300,000 is accepted by some as being the likely figure. He writes as follows:

> Nearly every plain, tableland and valley was inhabited for at least part of the year ... Among the areas which were closely settled were the banks and billabongs of the Murray River ... An anthropologist, A.R. Radcliffe-Brown, made the often-quoted estimate that Australia held an Aboriginal population of 250,000–300,000 at the time of the white man's arrival ...

These people were distributed among about 300 tribes and spoke altogether about 250 languages. Robert Hughes suggests that there may have been as many as 500 tribes or even perhaps as many as 900. Wikipedia suggests there may have been between 315,000 and 750,000 people, which is not a particularly helpful estimate.

The *Encyclopaedia Britannica* agrees that there may have been about 500 tribes, or 'sub-tribes' as this source calls them.

It also suggests there were about 300,000 people in number. It also refers to the Aboriginals as being 'semi-nomadic', which may be a helpful way of describing them while at the same time acknowledging their attachment to particular areas of land.

The continental landmass size of Australia is 7.688 million km². Assuming a population of 300,000, the land available for each Aboriginal inhabitant was thus 25.62 km², or 10.25 km² if the population was as high as 750,000 people.

It is worth reflecting how many small farms of, say, 20 acres (just over 8 ha) would fit into 10 km². The answer is about 125. An area of 20 acres would be a small farm area in a high productivity area (e.g. growing fruit trees). Typical large farms in grain-producing areas would probably number about 10.

The British did not use the doctrine of *terra nullius* or need to use it to create legal justification for a settlement in Australia. The idea that the British used this doctrine is often adopted by journalists and some academics, but it is not readily supported by any legal authority or historical records. The former Chief Justice of the High Court, Sir Harry Gibbs, had this to say on the subject in the Queensland Law Review, 1992:

> There is one matter which has puzzled me a little. In the judgements in Mabo, and in much public discussion which has followed, there are frequent references to the doctrine of terra nullius, which the Court is said to have rejected. The question whether land was terra nullius is relevant at international law in deciding whether a state has acquired sovereignty by attempted occupation. So far as I am aware, it was not the question asked at common law to determine

Chapter Seven The Aboriginals, their population and terra nullius

whether a colony, admittedly under the sovereignty of Great Britain, was acquired by settlement. Indeed the expression "terra nullius" seems to have been unknown to the common law. I have found no trace of it in legal dictionary ...

It was not mentioned in Tarring's Law relating to the Colonies (1913 ed.) which in its day was regarded as authoritative. It may have been thought to have been synonymous with the common law rule that if Englishmen establish themselves in an "uninhabited or barbarous country" the colony will be regarded as acquired by settlement but that ignores the fact that it was enough to satisfy the common law rule that the land was "barbarous" by which was meant not under civilised government. Australia was certainly not unoccupied in 1788 but it is another thing to say that the social organisation of the Aboriginal inhabitants was of a kind which the nations of Europe in the eighteenth and nineteenth centuries recognised as civilised. Of course, the High Court understood the full extent of the common law principles but public understanding is not assisted when those principles are described by a phrase which is misleading and perhaps emotive.

Whether they were sound laws or not, the results of the decisions in the Mabo and Wik cases created a legal position that made a big difference to the political scene and resulted in the legislation promoting native title.

The obvious legal position should surely be that the Crown, having taken the land away from its original occupants and occasional visitors, has legal control of that land and can order its disposition however it likes. That is really why native title requires to be governed by legislation. Without legislation, all such claims could be ignored from a strict legal perspective. Legally, the British thought the colony was 'settled' and not invaded. Since the Aboriginals did not have an obvious legal structure and did not seem to assert ownership in any way that was recognisable even among themselves, the British did not regard themselves as invaders. The Aboriginals really did believe they were being invaded, even if the invasion was not designed to be hostile in the sense that usually is thought to accompany invasion.

Commemorating the birth of Admiral Arthur Phillip in an address given in London on 14 October 2024, (reported in *The Australian*), Regius Professor Emeritus of Moral Theology at Oxford University Nigel Biggar spoke about the word 'invasion' in the context of the arrival of the First Fleet as follows:

> The word invasion misleads more than it illuminates. It connotes an intentional aggressiveness that was entirely lacking in 1788. It would be more appropriate to talk of an "intrusion". But intrusion, one way or another, sooner or later, was coming to Aboriginal Australia. And Phillip's was about the most fortunate the natives could have expected.

For a clear example of an invasion in that period, reference may be had to the invasion led by Horatio Nelson, then a Rear Admiral, in 1797, with 4000 men and 400 guns which was unsuccessful in conquering the Canary Islands which remained under Spanish rule. As has been said, the number of marines in the First Fleet was about 332. One marine died on the journey.

Chapter Seven The Aboriginals, their population and terra nullius

It is fairly clear that they did not consider themselves as an invasion force.

Phillip had been instructed to respect the native population. The instructions were contained in a document produced by the Home Office and stated that Phillip was to conduct matters as follows:

> ... to endeavour by every possible means to open an intercourse with the natives, and to conciliate their affections, enjoining all our subjects to live in amity and kindness with them and if any of our subjects shall wantonly destroy them, or give them any unnecessary interruption in the exercise of their several occupations, it is our will and pleasure that you do cause such offenders to be brought to punishment according to the degree of the offence.

Phillip himself added, 'any man who takes the life of a native will put on his trial the same as if he had killed one of the garrison'.

At the same time, it is reasonable to ask whether a handful of people moving about regularly over some hundreds of square kilometres every couple of years have thereby established a reasonable right to exclude others from the external ambit of that total area upon the basis of a legal title which, in almost all cases, was never formally claimed and which area of land was never clearly identifiable by any maps or markers anywhere other than in the knowledge and memory of the members of the local tribes. In addition, much of the land was regularly abandoned upon a basis of needs for food.

It is also quite clear that the original method of establishing rights of entry or control of an area of land by native people was frequently by armed conflict which continued into the twentieth century and was probably discontinued as the British legal system spread across the country and at the same time as the necessity for a nomadic lifestyle diminished.

Whatever the moral force of their position, it is difficult to see how one could say that the local tribal group or groups was capable of identification as a nation or even a state. One dictionary refers to a nation as a 'large group of people gathered as a state'. Another refers to an 'organised' group and having 'identifiable' land. One thing that can be said is that it is highly unlikely that any of the tribes regarded themselves as constituting a nation or a state. They thought of themselves no doubt as a tribe or family, as they would normally have been. Nowadays, I believe they are comfortable in referring to themselves not in a cynical way as 'members of our mob'.

It was a Canadian practice to describe tribal groups as First Nations, of which there are about 630 now in Canada. It is a peculiar concept to describe a small primitive tribe as a nation, in particular if they are nomadic, which it appears that the majority in Canada were not.

The three early eastern colonies established by the British at no stage appear to have suggested that their settlements constituted nations.

In a recent article in *The Spectator* magazine, the linguist, Kel Richards, wrote about the use of the expression 'First Nations' and his article included the following:

The term 'First Nations' was coined by Indian chiefs in

Ontario, Canada, in 1980. It seems to have been adopted by Aboriginal activists in Australia around 1995. It is what I call an 'aggrandisement' expression – trying to make Stone Age tribal life in Australia before 1788 sound far grander than it ever was ...

Before 1788 there were no 'nations' here – there were Stone Age, hunter-gatherer, nomadic tribes. They hadn't discovered metal working, they hadn't invented the wheel, they had no written language. They were not 'nations' in any sense of the word ... The other part of the expression is also troublesome. The word 'First' is used in order to belittle everyone else. It is a claim of priority. It is used to imply that everyone else is second.

It is quite reasonable for any observer to say that there may be moral rights which should be respected, but what do those moral rights dictate? We will return to this.

Chapter Eight

The lives of Aboriginals (men and women)

We have a few useful resources to help us understand Aboriginal life before the settlers came.

One author of importance is Watkin Tench who wrote two lengthy books about the settlement of New South Wales. Tench was an officer in the marines who accompanied the sailors and convicts on the First Fleet. Tench's work has been combined in the book, *1788*, produced and edited by Tim Flannery, who has made minor adjustments to spelling and punctuation to Tench's narrative but is confident that the text is given as first published in the eighteenth century.

Flannery says that, 'Tench was a friend and confidante of the Aboriginals who attached themselves to the settlement. He learned their language and they, apparently, reposed full confidence in him'.

Tench arrived back in England in 1792. He made numerous observations about the Aboriginals, some of whom he clearly admired. Contrary to the shameful nonsense provided by the infamous Bruce Pascoe, Tench records about the natives that, 'to cultivation of the ground they are utter strangers'. This is an

Chapter Eight The lives of Aboriginals (men and women)

important issue in dealing with Aboriginals.

In the journals of Joseph Banks, who was one of Captain Cook's biologists, it states: 'We never saw one inch of cultivated land in the whole country.'

James Burney, being a member of Captain Cook's first voyage, recorded while in Tasmania the following observation about the natives:

> ... one of these gentlemen, whether sitting, walking or talking, will pour forth his streams without any preparatory action or guidance, or even appearing sensible of what he was doing, and not in the least interested whether it trickles down his own thighs or sprinkles the person next to him.

One might have thought it obvious that excreta, whether of fluids or solids, might be dealt with as waste and not supposed to be attached to or poured upon humans after emerging.

Upon the subject of cannibalism, Tench stated , 'There is no reason to suppose that these people [the eastern coastal tribes] were cannibals. Nor do they ever eat animal substances in a raw state unless pressed by extreme hunger.'

Yet William Buckley, the convict who lived with native tribes for thirty years, had no doubts about cannibalism and described cannibalistic practices in Western Victoria. He had this to say:

> ... the truth must prevail ... that many of the natives inhabiting this part of the continent of New Holland are cannibals, under particular circumstances, cannot be doubted ...
>
> The cause of this ... cruelty was ... [a] man who was killed by the bite of a snake belonged to [a] hostile tribe, and they

believed my supposed brother-in-law carried about with him something that had occasioned his death. They have all sorts of fancies of this kind, and it is frequently the case that they take a man's kidneys out after his death, tie them up in something, and carry them round the neck, as a sort of ... charm ...

... the mangled remains [of a young man's body] were roasted between heated stones, shared out, and greedily devoured ... Again I was pressed to join in this horrid repast; but I hope I need not say, that I refused, with indignation and disgust ...

It is true that they are cannibals – I have seen them eat small portions of the flesh of their adversaries slain in battle ... they also eat of the flesh of their own children to whom they have been much attached should they die a natural death.

Considering the autobiography of William Buckley, it is worthy of recording the independent comments about the creditability of the accounts which he records in his book. Tim Flannery, who had in 2002 produced the recent publication of the book first published in 1852 and wrote an introduction to the book, discusses the creditability of the work as follows:

Despite its cool reception by some, "Life and Adventures" has been received creditably by experts over the years. Edward Carr, author of "The Australian Race" (1886), was one who knew traditional Aboriginal societies well. "I think I am right to say," he wrote, "that Morgan's 'Life and Adventures of William Buckley' gives a truer account of Aboriginal life

Chapter Eight The lives of Aboriginals (men and women)

than any work I have read." More recently Marjorie Tipping who wrote Buckley's entry in the Australian Dictionary of Biography, noted that "Life and Adventures" is "close to fact" while an anthropologist L.R. Hiatt has said (in personal communication), "There is a much higher degree of consistency with modern understanding of Aboriginal life ... than inconsistency."

Tench describes the practice of cutting off the two lower joints of the little finger of the left hand among the women, 'who have for the most part undergone this amputation'. The coastal tribesmen also extracted a single tooth on the left side of the mouth which, it seems, that they also practised upon women when they were being married.

Professor Blainey wrote that '... abortions, warfare, the killing of unwanted babies, and the inability to care for the old were persistent obstacles to the rapid rise of [Aboriginal] population.'

On the subject of inter-tribal conflict, Tench wrote:

From circumstances which have been observed, we have sometimes been inclined to believe these people at war with each other... An officer one day met fourteen of them marching along in a regular Indian file through the woods, each man armed with a spear in his right hand and a large stone in his left.

Professor Blainey made a careful analysis of the details provided by William Buckley concerning conflicts among tribes and decided that 'the reported deaths represented a high ratio of casualties. Moreover the massacres and ambushes so far culled from his reminiscences might well have happened in his first year with the Aboriginals ... Even if those violent deaths ... had been spread over thirty years instead of one year they would have underlined the effect of warfare on a small population.'

Looking at the information about the conflicts in Arnhem Land, Professor Blainey concluded that:

> ... Even the direct drain on Japan's population through the loss of fighting men in (all) theatres of war between 1937 and 1945 was not quite as high as warfare's drain on the population of Arnhem Land ... warfare was one of the powerful curbs on the growth of population.

About the treatment of their women by the Aboriginals, Tench had this to say:

> ... indeed the women are in all respects treated with savage barbarity. Condemned not only to carry the children but all other burdens they met in return for submission only with blows, kicks and every other mark of brutality. When an Indian (*sic.*, a native male) is provoked by a woman, he either spears her or knocks her down on the spot. On this occasion he always strikes on the head, using indiscriminately a hatchet, a club or any other weapon which may chance to be in his hand ... Colbee (a native befriended by Tench) ... made no scruple of treating [his wife] thus ...
>
> A thousand times I have wished that those European philosophers, whose closest speculations exalt a state of nature above a state of civilisation, could survey the phantom which their heated imaginations have raised.

Chapter Eight The lives of Aboriginals (men and women)

In modern Australia, we know such philosophising about the call of native 'culture' echoes Tench's reflections of over two hundred years ago.

Paleopathologist Stephen Webb in 1995 published his analysis of 4500 individuals' bones from mainland Australia going back 50,000 years. Webb found highly disproportionate rates of injuries and fractures to women's skulls, with the injuries suggesting deliberate attacks and often attacks from behind, perhaps in domestic squabbles. In the tropics, for example, female head injury frequency was twenty to thirty-three per cent versus six and a half to twenty per cent for males. The most extreme results were on the south coast from Swanport and Adelaide, with formal cranial trauma rates as high as forty to forty-four per cent, two to four times the rate of male cranial trauma. In desert and south coast areas, five to six per cent of female skulls had three separate head injuries and eleven to twelve per cent had two injuries. Webb could not rule out women-to-women attacks but thought that less probable. His findings, according to anthropologist Peter Sutton, confirm that serious armed assaults were common in Australia over thousands of years prior to the settlements by the British.

Aboriginal women must, at some stage, have cheered the coming of the British. If they did not, they must have enjoyed pain and suffering. There must also be a residual sadness that many Aboriginal men can still behave towards women as if the laws do not apply to them. Of course, it is now reflected clearly in the level of imprisonment of Aboriginal men because of domestic violence.

In his book published in 1882, titled *Old Colonials*, AJ Boyd tells us as follows:

> Their manner of treating their women ... is most barbarous. Only a few hours ago I was an eye witness of the semi-murder (if there be such an offence) of a gin, within twenty yards of my own house. A blackfellow, after bandying high words with his gin, deliberately raised his tomahawk and cracked her skull with the utmost coolness. About a dozen other blacks were standing round, and the only remark was "My word, Budgeree hit 'im that fellow". The gin dropped like a log, drenched with blood, and was removed to the camp.

(Other reports by Boyd are in a later chapter.)

It is quite obvious that part of Aboriginal culture was the serious subjugation of women which continued throughout the nineteenth century, and the effects of that attitude persist today in the appalling statistics of domestic violence in remote communities.

In an article in *The Australian* of 22 January 2020, a speech given by Jacinta Nampijinpa Price is reported with the following extracts:

> With 23% of partner homicides being indigenous, it is not time to worry about ... "changing the date". Vast amounts of money are spent every year on addressing this issue yet very little appears to be achieved in reducing the rates of violence and death ... Our Watch is another organisation promoting (this) view that Aboriginal perpetrators of violence are themselves victims of the brutality of colonisation and therefore cannot take full responsibility for their actions ...

Chapter Eight The lives of Aboriginals (men and women)

> Such conclusions are not reflective of the experience of we Aboriginal women who have survived within the confines of traditional Aboriginal culture ... As a girl growing up I saw other girls my age reach adolescence and then be married off to much older men while still too young to be legally married under Australian law ... I witnessed women being brutally beaten by their husbands, but the cultural acceptance of it was so strong no one outside my immediate family supported the victim or reported the abuse ... One has only to look up the book on Ngarra law to understand not only how traditional Yolngu law accepts violence against women ... Surely a girl 13 to 16 years old cannot be considered able to become a wife to a man aged 40 or 50 ... Is it not a human rights violation to spear a girl of 13 to 16 through the leg should she be found guilty of breaking traditional cultural law? ... Indigenous partner homicide rates are high ... because of the underlying cultural forces that perpetuate the family violence epidemic.

As to the present situation in remote Aboriginal communities, the comments by Senator Price are supported by, among others, Dr Kirsten Due, whose work as a doctor in remote communities is discussed in an article in *The Australian* magazine section of 6–7 July 2024, and includes the following:

> Nearly every clinic I've been to has been attacked with crowbars or rammed with stolen 4×4s by people adrift in a wilderness. Their lives have driven them to soothe distressed neurons by petrol and solvent sniffing. People demanding money or drugs. Or wanting access to an injured

female patient so they can beat her up (again). Or violent offenders who have become psychotic (again) since release from prison. Every remote doctor or nurse knows someone who has been threatened, if not assaulted.

Chapter Nine

Aboriginal deaths from conflicts

According to Professor Henry Reynolds, a prominent advocate for Aboriginals, the number of Aboriginals killed by the British in the period from 1788 to 1938 was probably about 30,000. (He had previously estimated 20,000 but reacted to what he accepted as additional emerging evidence). It is worthy of passing note that a certain number of these were killed by Aboriginal trackers employed by the British. The total represents about 200 deaths per year. Among those killed were those who were in the process of attacking white settlers who were defending themselves from Aboriginal attacks. It is not always appropriate to be calling some of these encounters 'massacres' when some of the engagements were, in reality, battles, regardless of the issue of rights.

The *Guardian*, a left-wing news outlet, maintains that between 11,000 and 14,000 Aboriginals died but only 390 to 440 colonisers. Taking the higher figure, the resulting annual figure of deaths from this analysis would be 93.

A project headed by historian Lyndall Ryan from the University of Newcastle, funded by the Australian Research

Council, has been researching and mapping the sites of massacres. A massacre is defined for this study as 'the deliberate and unlawful killing of six or more undefended people in one operation', and an interactive map has been developed. As of 16 November 2021, an estimated 304 massacres had been recorded as having taken place in the period between 1788 and 1930. As of 2022, the number of documented massacres of Aboriginal and Torres Strait Islander people have risen to 412. The number of deaths of Aboriginals from settler conflicts was estimated at between 10,000 and 11,000. A figure of 11,000 provides a yearly total of 73 over the 150-year period from 1788 to 1938.

If this rate is applied across the total population of Aboriginals, and if that total was 300,000, then the number is 1 in every 4100 Aboriginals. If the population was 750,000, the number is 1 in every 10,274 people.

In general, the killing of Aboriginals by the British was not the direct result of government policy. In fact, the famous Myall Creek massacre of Aboriginals in 1838 by white men became famous not because of the murder of the Aboriginals but because seven of the non-indigenous men accused and found guilty of the murders were hanged. This was a rare but important occurrence. It would be interesting to know if there was a similar case in the colonies of other countries.

One can compare that sad total of deaths, though, with the loss of life by Australian soldiers (including some Aboriginals) in the two world wars. As noted previously, in the four years of the Great War, Australia lost 62,000 directly by death. In World War II, the loss over six years was 40,464. Later deaths of returned soldiers who died or whose lives were shortened by injuries or death are not recorded.

The first 'massacre' was reported in the *Sydney Gazette* on 6 April 1806 when it revealed that the crew of the *George*, a sailing vessel, killed nine Aboriginal people at Twofold Bay. It is reported that:

> ... a whole body showed themselves, with a determined resolution to attack the gang en masse. They advanced with shouts and menaces until within reach of a spear, several of which were thrown; and then the gang, eleven in number, in self defence commenced to fire by which nine of the assailants were laid prostrate whereupon all the rest made off.

As mentioned previously, Professor Blainey discusses the inter-tribal conflicts which were a regular part of tribal life before the arrival of the British. He says this about the experiences of William Buckley living with Aboriginals in southern Victoria:

> If we go on to accept a very cautious estimate of the number of fighting deaths, we arrive at the conclusion that the (annual) death rate in warfare equalled 1 for every 270 in the population. That death rate was probably not exceeded in any nation of Europe during any of the last three centuries.
>
> Two thousand miles to the north an American anthropologist, Lloyd Warner, studying in the twilight of tribal life, collected many details of Aboriginals dying in warfare during a period of twenty years ... Warner concluded that a total of 200 men died from organized warfare in north-east Arnhem Land between 1909 and 1929.

This latter figure emerges from a population of some 3000

people in the area, so the average annual death rate was 1 in every 300 people.

It is, of course, a speculation that these fair estimates made by academics in relation to two areas in completely different parts of Australia are typical. They may be unsound in either direction; that is, they may have been a great deal more or a lot less. However, subject to that qualification, it is clear from various sources and experiences that it is not unreasonable to use the figures as a guide to the behaviour of the population at large. Thus, transferring these figures to the population at large would have meant that the *annual* death rate from Aboriginal warfare (at 1 in every 300 in Arnhem Land) would have been about 1000 in a total population of 300,000, or about 2500 in a population of 750,000. At the rate of 1 in every 270 (in Western Victoria), the figures would have been 1110 in a population of 300,000 and 2777 in a population of 750,000.

The comparison is stark. The rate of deaths from tribal conflicts is substantially greater than deaths from settler conflicts.

One serious encounter was recorded by Assistant Protector Charles Wightman Sievwright in April 1841 in what is now part of the State of Victoria. When there was fierce hand-to-hand fighting between two Aboriginal tribes, more than a hundred warriors exchanged spears, boomerangs and other weapons in clashes lasting about three hours. Many male fighters received spear wounds. He was unable to learn what the fight was about, because they could not speak his language and he could not speak theirs.

Another tribal battle was described by anthropologist TGH Strehlow. It occurred in 1875 in the Finke River area of Central Australia. He wrote:

> The warriors turned their murderous attention to the women and older children and either clubbed them or speared them to death. Finally, according to the grim custom of warriors and avengers they broke the limbs of the infants, leaving them to die "natural deaths". The final number of the dead could well have reached the high figure of 80 to 100 men, women and children.

Just to repeat, based on the estimates of Professor Reynolds of 30,000, the death rate from settler conflicts per annum was 200, or based on Professor Ryan of 11,000 was 93. In a population of 300,000, the death rate was 1 in every 1500 for Professor Reynolds and 1 in every 3000+ for Professor Ryan. In a population of 750,000, the death rates would have been one in every 3750 for Professor Reynolds and one in every 8000+ for Professor Ryan.

Placing the figure for colonial conflicts between whites and Aboriginals in the same context as the deaths from warfare among tribes helps to understand that, while the history of the conflicts is a very sad and tragic one, it is fair to say that in some ways it could have been a great deal worse. Bear in mind that the Incas lost 2000 people in one day in South America and ultimately the whole of their huge empire was destroyed by the year 1572, although they began their relationship with the Spaniards with an army of 80,000 Inca men.

In the United States, the loss of life for native Americans

was enormous. Some millions of people were reduced to a few hundred thousand. There were apparently some official 1500 instances of wars, attacks and raids by settlers upon the native tribes. In addition, it seems to have been a common practice for settlers to make a treaty with native Americans and then to break its terms.

A book on the subject of tribal warfare is titled *War Before Civilization: The Myth of the Peaceful Savage* by Lawrence H. Keeley who is Professor of Archaeology at University of Illinois in Chicago. The author conducts an investigation of the archaeological evidence for prehistoric violence, including murders and massacres as well as war. He maintains that peaceful societies are exceptional. About ninety to ninety-five per cent engage in war. The attrition rate of numerous close-quarter clashes, which characterise warfare in tribal warrior society, produces casualty rates of up to sixty per cent compared to one per cent of combatants as is typical in modern warfare. Evidence shows that tribal warfare is on average twenty times more deadly than twentieth-century warfare. Included in examples is a reference to the same study of deaths in a given period in Arnhem Land to which Professor Blainey has referred. The author points out that over the period of twenty years studied, about twenty-five per cent of all males had been killed.

Professor Keeley supports the analysis made above about the level of tribal warfare in Australia among Aboriginals, which was conspicuously a great deal more than the deaths from conflicts with settlers. The reality passed over by most is that the deaths from settler conflicts were simply not that many in the normal expectation of life, death and fighting for Aboriginals.

Of course, this analysis is incomplete in that it does not say a great deal about the debilitating impact of the settlers upon the lives of Aboriginals, nor about the impacts of disease which is discussed in the next chapter.

Chapter Ten

The impact of disease

Of course, it is generally acknowledged that the more substantial killer of Aboriginals than conflicts with settlers was the introduction of diseases. In early eighteenth-century Europe, the annual death rate from smallpox was variously reported as being between 200,000 and 300,000 people. In one year alone in the city of Paris, 20,000 deaths occurred.

Edward Jenner developed the practice of vaccination but his major findings occurred as late as 1796. This procedure involved infecting a patient with cowpox which resulted in immunity from smallpox. Before this, the practice had developed of infecting patients with a small dose of smallpox which would ultimately give immunity from the disease. This procedure was known as variolation. The negative effect of this procedure was that a small percentage of people thus treated died from the effect of the treatment. On balance, it was probably still preferable to use the procedure than not do so.

The doctors who travelled on the First Fleet had some samples of the virus which presumably were to be made available for use to produce immunity.

At least a year after the settlement by the First Fleet, there was a fatal outbreak of the disease among the coastal tribes of

Chapter Ten The impact of disease

natives. Large numbers of them died.

Watkin Tench made several comments in his books on the subject. Before relaying those, it is well worth the mention of an encounter which took place in April 1791. In this passage, Tench is speaking about a man met on one of several expeditions away from the settlement in various groups that sometimes included the governor. On this occasion, while crossing a creek, the party encountered members of another tribe a long way from the settlement, including this particular individual. Tench reports as follows:

> ... a native, from his canoe, entered into conversation with us, and immediately after, paddled to us with a frankness and confidence which surprised everyone. He was a man of middle age, with an open and cheerful countenance marked with the smallpox, and distinguished by a nose of uncommon magnitude and dignity.

It is clear that Tench was a person of considerable intellectual ability. It is improbable that he was mistaken about this, as the signs of smallpox must have been quite common in his previous experiences, and he was an astute observer.

About the smallpox visited upon the coastal tribes, Tench reports that in April 1789, bodies of the 'Indians' were being found in all the coves and inlets of the harbour. On inspection by the medical people in the settlement, he says:

> ... it appeared that all the parties had died a natural death. Pustules similar to those being caused by smallpox were thickly spread on the bodies, but how a disease to which our former observations had led us to suppose them strangers

could have introduced itself, and have spread so widely, seemed inexplicable.

After recounting some experiences with the diseased people, Tench wrote:

> No solution of this difficulty had been given when I left the colony in December 1791. I can therefore only propose queries for the ingenuity of others to exercise itself upon: is it a disease indigenous to the country? Did the French ships under Monsieur La Perouse introduce it? Let it be remembered that they had now been departed more than a year and we had never heard of its existence on board of them ...
>
> No person among us had been afflicted with the disorder since we had quitted the Cape of Good Hope seventeen months before. It is true that our surgeons had brought out variolous matter in bottles, but to infer that it was produced from this cause were a supposition so wild as to be unworthy of consideration.

While it is convenient to suppose that the disease was introduced by the First Fleet, the evidence presented by Tench seems to make that improbable. In addition, the existence of a man from a more remote tribe who had obviously had the disease and survived would seem to indicate that the introduction may have had another source.

We may never know.

It has been suggested that the Aboriginals may have come into contact with smallpox from Indonesian sailors visiting the north of Australia. It has also been suggested that the virus was deliberately passed on to the Aboriginals to kill them off. This seems rather bizarre and extremely unlikely. The convicts were apparently mainly illiterate. How would they have obtained the samples of the virus? If they did come across samples, we cannot imagine their first thought would have been to handle them in any way. They were not highly educated, in the main.

It appears that the Aboriginals were highly vulnerable to the foreign disease, and this seems a good explanation of the devastation they suffered. Professor Blainey suggests that the Aboriginals may have experienced epidemics in earlier years which would help to explain the low population growth. Some other obvious reasons for a lack of population growth might include the fact that about 30% of all newborn babies were killed at birth. Among others, if twins were born, one was always dispatched. Children with a deformity were always killed.

Judy Campbell taught in the Department of History at Australian National University. Her book on the subject is titled *Invisible Invader: Smallpox and other diseases in Aboriginal Australia 1780-1880*. While it is likely that tuberculosis was introduced into Australia with the First Fleet, she considers it not likely that smallpox was introduced by the First Fleet. Her lengthy book on the subject shows a well-researched understanding. A few of her comments are quoted as follows:

> Smallpox and tuberculosis were unknown to the indigenous inhabitants of the isolated continents of America and Australia, and they were the most damaging of new infectious diseases to break out among Native Americans and Aboriginal Australians when their isolation ended.

Smallpox travelled with English settlers and their African slaves on the short Atlantic crossing in the seventeenth century. In the late eighteenth and nineteenth centuries many migrants leaving for North America and Australia were heavily infected with tuberculosis, because England was then at the height of an epidemic of the disease.

Although members of the First Fleet soon realized that "consumption" had travelled to Australia with them, they were certain that smallpox had not ... occurred in any members of the First Fleet. Not long after 1800 most European travellers arriving in Australia had been vaccinated. However, colonists and convicts from England were not the only voyagers to arrive in Australia between 1780 and 1870 and there were widespread outbreaks of smallpox among Aboriginals in those years.

... [Northern Territory Aboriginals] had contact with travellers from islands in the Indonesian archipelago, who regularly visited them. These travellers were Macassan fishermen from South Sulawesi and neighbouring islands ... and reliable observers attributed Aboriginal smallpox to contact with the travellers from the north.

... Smallpox was followed by tuberculosis among Aboriginals who [clearly] had contact with Europeans in newly settled districts in south-eastern Australia.

According to Professor Blainey, another significant cause of death was occasioned by the wearing of wet clothes or lying on wet blankets, both of which caused hundreds of deaths from chills, influenza and pneumonia. Wearing clothes made of cloth or sleeping on blankets were generally unknown in pre-colonial days.

William Buckley spoke of another illness:

> A syphilis disorder is very prevalent among them not only the adults but the children. Promiscuous intercourse of the sexes is not uncommon and in certain festivals is enjoined – at certain times the women are lent to the young men who have not wives.

Venereal disease became widespread in Victoria and New South Wales among Aboriginal women who were often prostituted to settlers and squatters, in particular during and after the gold rushes.

While Buckley appears to have been quite credible with his autobiographical history of his many years with the native tribes, it is possible that his comment about syphilis may have been reflective of an emergence of the disease somewhat later. According to Dr Harris in his book on the missionaries (which is discussed later), venereal disease was rampant in Victoria and New South Wales sometime before, and then during, the gold rush period. It appears to have had a devastating impact on Aboriginal women. Mercury was used as a treatment for syphilis, but it was probably not available to Aboriginals.

William Buckley recalls how while he was with the Aboriginals, another infection once swept through the countryside, taking many lives and causing ulcerous sores and swelling of feet.

This occurrence raises the question as to whether epidemics have sometimes emerged from a source within Australia, and it does seem to be at least possible. Professor Blainey writes that it is believed that Murray Valley encephalitis was carried south by migrating birds and then been widely spread by mosquitoes.

Chapter Eleven

The invasion or settlement

By the standards of the time, the British can be judged firstly as having done nothing unusual. In general, they also did not think their position was an immoral one. The view that it was an immoral and improper intrusion developed over time and in the light of the inability of the two races to reach an acceptable form of agreement. The traditional way of life of the Aboriginals was frequently destroyed by the settlers, but it was believed that the Aboriginal life was uncivilised, irreligious and not worthy of retention, in particular in relation to the treatment of women. There was fundamental misunderstanding on both sides.

The British brought Christianity to the Aboriginals, and that was regarded as a matter of importance and expected to be beneficial. For some Aboriginals, it did prove to be beneficial, even if it was only simply in the fact that various religious groups brought education to a number of Aboriginals, including lepers. This included a cousin of this author who was a nun in Western Australia teaching Aboriginals for over sixty years. Like this author, she was also descended from members of the First Fleet. (She is mentioned in this book again in a later chapter.)

Some parts of the Aboriginal life changed by the settlers were clearly beneficial. The practices of cannibalism, infanticide and polygamy widely practised by Aboriginals disappeared over time.

As has been said, it appears that among many Aboriginal tribes, about 30% of children were killed at birth. According to Professor Blainey, occasionally a younger child was killed so that its flesh could be fed to an older child. You may recall that the first settlers were shocked when an Aborigine smashed the head of a baby whose mother had died and buried the baby with the mother. When they remonstrated with the man responsible, he asked the question as to who would have been able to care for the child. No doubt this approach reflected the nomadic influence on life. It seems likely that infanticide was very widespread. Abortion was also common, but abortion is not a crime in Australia now and is of course very common. One common feature of Aboriginal life in present-day Australia among remote tribes is the practice of incest and paedophilia. Both of these practices are crimes in Australia.

The precise extent of these practices is unknown, but Professor Blainey states there is convincing evidence that in a number of districts, Aboriginals committed murder to eat the flesh of the victims. He also states that there are reports (some false) of Aboriginals who ate the flesh of people who had died peacefully. In relation to cannibalism, the reality may be that the practice was common in some areas and not others.

Equally, polygamy may have been common in some areas but not others. In a neighbouring tribe to the coastal tribes, Tench learned that every male member of the tribe had two wives. Women in Aboriginal communities obviously did not enjoy a lot of respect from men. You will recall that the women were sometimes offered by one tribe to another as sexual objects as well as being offered to the whites. In some cases, it is believed that if such an offer was refused, it could lead to warfare. Women were also suppressed in many other parts of the world but in Europe less so than elsewhere, and the 2023 Women, Peace and Security Index indicated that Australia may now be one of the best places in the world for the rights of women.

Professor Blainey says that polygamy was widely practised and that in the north-east of Arnhem Land, 'the average middle-aged man had three or four wives'. However, it is possible that Aboriginal women, while treated poorly, were probably relatively not dramatically worse off than some Muslim women in the twentieth century in some Muslim-dominated countries.

As well as the population being limited by the frequent killing of newborn children, there is also some evidence that not a lot of respect was awarded towards the aged among the population.

Professor Blainey tells about an explorer leading an expedition south of Alice Springs in 1873 who came across a tribe at a waterhole which included an elderly and infirm woman. A member of the party, having pity for the woman, boiled some flour to make gruel and gave it to the woman. Other members of the tribe reacted with negative sentiments about the gift and asked what was the point of feeding her, as she was going to die. It is fair to say that the nomadic lifestyle did not allow for serious regard for the elderly. If you were old and lacked mobility, you were left behind when a tribe moved on.

Professor Blainey also suggests quite reasonably that the values by which the conduct of Aboriginals might be judged are not eternal, and often dictates of circumstances are quite different for different societies.

In the long run, the British put an end to tribal warfare which, as can be seen from the figures mentioned above, caused many unnatural deaths among Aboriginals. In addition, some of the more violent aspects of Aboriginal culture, including some violent superstitious practices, largely disappeared.

The Aboriginals ultimately benefited from many things, both physical and otherwise, provided by the British, including the following:

- reading, writing and arithmetic
- books, schools and education
- cooking skills and the use of many tools not previously available
- buildings including houses, churches, schools, universities and libraries
- clothing (cotton and wool)
- domestic animals (cows, sheep, horses) camels
- hospitals
- bridges
- vehicles including those with wheels
- cultivation of crops including grains, fruit and vegetables
- furniture
- sailing ships
- most musical instruments
- weapons

- machinery including windmills
- telescopes.

In relation to arithmetic, the coastal Aboriginals only counted to four. For anything greater than four, they would use a word meaning 'great' and for a very big number, they would add 'great, great' in their language.

One may also reflect upon the huge changes to the human experience brought about by European and Western developments in the period subsequent to British settlement, developments in which the Aboriginals shared; for example, photography, radio, television, films, trains, motorised and other vehicles, aeroplanes, telephones, electric lighting, refrigeration and computers, to name a few. Obviously, if their partly nomadic lifestyle had remained undisturbed by settlers, it is difficult to imagine that any of these inventions would have been available to them at all until imported by other settlers.

Of course, it is clear that the Europeans also brought disease which was almost certainly the worst killer of Aboriginals. One of the worst aspects of serious illness was that a tribe would blame another tribe for the illnesses and take revenge by attacking them. (You may recall the extraordinary practice of 'pointing the bone' at some opponent with the intention that it would cause that opponent's death.)

Aboriginals were ultimately able to enjoy the benefits of a legal system and government that provided democracy and personal rights. Inter-tribal conflicts were largely eliminated, but not until the twentieth century. It is worthy of note to mention that Aboriginal women in the State of South Australia were among the first females to be able to vote in elections anywhere in the world. In fact, in many parts of Europe and elsewhere, only men were permitted to vote at that time, and many men had no such right.

It should not be overlooked that Aboriginals also brought some useful talents to the mix. In particular, they made a substantial contribution to the early settlers and their exploration of both the interior and the country at large. Matthew Flinders was accompanied on his trip around Australia by a well-regarded and competent Aboriginal named Bungaree. The early explorers reached a stage of appreciation of the Aboriginal trackers to the extent that many considered it unwise to travel without one in the party who had the common Aboriginal skills pertaining to the water, the land and its flora and fauna.

Chapter Twelve

Violence towards the settlers

It has been mentioned that, quite early in the settlement, members of the First Fleet were murdered by the Aboriginals. This occurred mainly when convicts or marines were on their own or in a very small group. As has been told, Governor Phillip was also speared by a native. At the time, he was taken back to the settlement, and fearing his imminent death, he made his will. Happily, he recovered.

There are reports of killings by Aboriginals of white settlers, in particular when the settlers were on their own or comprised a married couple on their own.

William Alexander Jenyns (AJ) Boyd was born in 1842 and moved to Queensland as a young man. For a few years, he was headmaster of Toowoomba Grammar School. Later, he became editor of the *Queensland Agricultural Journal*, a position he held for over thirty years. His book, *Old Colonials*, was published in London in 1882. He had a low opinion of Aboriginal males and described them as follows:

> As for the Australian blackfellow … his virtues and heroism must have been "dreamed of in dream", for a personal acquaintance with the noble savage in his native wilds [my opinion of him is] that he is, when stripped of poetic imagery,

nothing but a sneaking, filthy, thievish, murdering vagabond – a very Cain, whose hand is against every man, and every man's hand against him ... Too lazy to work themselves they evidence their nobility of soul by compelling their wretched gins to perform all the drudgery. The noble savages content themselves with carrying their weapons and occasionally indulging in the pastime of knocking down a gin with a blow from a nullah-nullah.

Boyd recounts the story of an attack upon the settlers by the natives:

A man and his wife lived together on a small farm about 15 miles from a northern township. The blacks in that part of the country had always been noted for their cunning, ferocity and hatred of the white man, and the farmer had often been entreated to abandon so dangerous a locality ... however the farmer had allowed the natives to visit his dwelling and had constantly fed them ... feeling that gratitude would surely deter them from injuring them ... for weeks the blacks had been [making preparations] ... On a certain day the savages mustered at the farm in greater numbers than usual ... This gave the farmer no uneasiness ... At a moment when his back was turned a spear was driven through his back ... [they] then fell on him, and despatched him with nullah-nullahs ...The terrified wife ... seized a double-barrelled gun [she] pulled both triggers, but the caps misfired. She turned to fly [but] was overtaken and mercilessly hewn down ...

A day or two afterwards a gin was taken in the act of gnawing one of the feet of the slaughtered man, whilst other

Chapter Twelve Violence towards the settlers

half-roasted portions of the body were found in her dilly bag ... [the] tribe had been unmolested by the whites and had [been camped in the area for some time].

Another instance of the murder of whites by blacks in Queensland involved the father of Tom Wills who was one of the main, if not the most important, founders of Australian Rules football. A group of warriors attacked the party while they were establishing camp. Wills senior had a gun but not on his person, and not suspecting the intention of the native, had not thought it necessary to try to retrieve it before he was murdered. It was thought that the attack was a reprisal in response to an earlier attack on the tribe by whites, but those involved in that earlier encounter had no connection with the Wills family group who thought to befriend the natives.

Chapter Thirteen

The missionaries

The harsh reality is that the native tribes and the European settlers were never going to be able to live together in harmony. The differences were too profound. When the settlers sowed plants which grew, the natives would remove them as they were simply part of the growth which they had always harvested on what they considered their land. They did not seek permission nor thought it necessary. The settlers thought of them as thieves and reacted accordingly. The natives would never have been able to appreciate the views of the settlers. The settlers did not understand the natives and thought them primitive, which they were by European standards, but of course they had their own customs.

The natives were overwhelmed by dispossession when the settlers used land allocated to them by the distant government or took land that they considered freely available to them. The natives were used to violence, but they were not generally equipped to resist the settlers, apart from being devious and cunning in some encounters.

The natives had no previous experience of tobacco or alcohol. As they were natural hunters and gatherers, they tended to consume what was available with the habits to which they were accustomed, including eating plenty when plenty was available. For example, when they were offered medicine, and if they accepted it as beneficial, they would consume all that was available or provided. There was no custom of taking a bit each day for a week.

An important book based on the missions is titled *One Blood: 200 years of Aboriginal encounter with Christianity: a story of hope*. The main title is taken from the bible's Acts of the Apostles (17:26-28) and in the King James version, it appears as follows: 'And He has made from one blood every nation of men to dwell on all the face of the earth, and has determined their pre-appointed times and the boundaries of their dwellings ...' The book's author, John W. Harris, is an ordained Anglican minister and holds a PhD in Aboriginal languages. It is an impressive and very large volume covering a great deal of the dispossession of the Aboriginals and the work of the Christian missionaries.

A large number of missions were established in Australia in the early part of the nineteenth century with good intentions on their part in the main to introduce Christianity to the native population. Almost without exception, they failed dismally and closed down. A serious difficulty concerned language. One group of priests were German and did not speak English. Some worked hard to learn an Aboriginal language but since there were between 150 and 250 different languages, learning one Aboriginal language gave one the ability to communicate with relatively few natives, and that was before they could start to discuss theological concepts.

Some missions thrived due mainly to the strength of

character and commitment of their leaders. Dr Harris makes a very brief reference to an order of nuns. On page 471 of his book, he mentions the assistance to the Pallottines in Broome by 'a fine group of Irish St John of God nuns under Mother Antonia O'Brien'.

As has been mentioned previously, this author's cousin joined the order while still in her teens in the 1920s and taught Aboriginals in the order's schools and missions for over sixty years. Her name was Thelma Doolan. Her name in religion was Sister Therese so she was known as Sister Mary Therese Doolan. Her mother was originally Mary (or May) Lucas, the sister of this author's father. She entered the order at the age of fifteen in 1930. She died in 2004. Thelma taught school at Broome, at Beagle Bay mission and at the leper colony at Derby which was mainly a hospital conducted by the order. The order remains prominent in hospitals and schools in Western Australia.

An early missionary in New South Wales was Lancelot Threlkeld who represented the London Missionary Society. The first book of the bible to be translated into an Aboriginal language was the Gospel of Luke in 1830. He wrote: 'This translation of the Gospel of Luke into the language of the Aboriginals was made by me with the assistance of the intelligent Aboriginal, McGill ... [who] spoke the English language fluently ...' The language was Awabakal. His work was not published during his lifetime largely because there were so few speakers of that language left. His mission was at Port Macquarie, but it closed down and he moved to Sydney.

The fate of Aboriginals in Tasmania is known widely. The

Chapter Thirteen The missionaries

remnant of the natives, after a lot of killing, were persuaded to be removed to Flinders Island in Bass Strait where they declined even further.

In Victoria, as in New South Wales, all early efforts at establishing missions failed. A school was established at Merri Creek on the outskirts of Melbourne by the Baptists for Aboriginal children. It had some success but ultimately had to be closed. At one stage, young girls would be attending classes when their much older husbands would come to take them away to allow the older partner to exercise his marital rights.

In the latter part of the nineteenth century, several missions were established and provided support to Aboriginals who were at that stage in serious need of assistance. In Gippsland, there were two major missions in operation: one was at Lake Tyers, another was nearby. There was also an operating mission in the Wimmera in north-western Victoria.

In one mission, the manager required the Aboriginals to surrender their spears and other weapons. At Lake Tyers, the Aboriginals seeking assistance and support, voluntarily surrendered their weapons.

The settlement at Lake Tyers survived until 1971 when the government handed it over with an accompanying large parcel of land to a trust for the benefit of the Aboriginals. The year before, in 1970, this author visited the place with his family and found a relatively recently built building housing large rooms, bathrooms and toilets. Every piece of wood or metal that could be removed had been removed from the building. There appeared then to be no person living there.

One of several successful mission houses was in New Norcia in Western Australia, about 130 kilometres from Perth. It was established in 1847 and still houses monks. The sad reality is that abuse of children during later years was common and was the subject of legal claims which were settled by the Catholic Church. It is fair to say that this mission had contributed greatly to the benefit of Aboriginals in earlier times.

Among the missionaries were a number who took the trouble to learn a local Aboriginal language and to develop a written version of that language.

Part Four
The stolen generation and compensation for loss

Chapter Fourteen

The stolen generation

The 'Bringing Them Home' Report was tabled in Federal Parliament in 1997. The report considered that the forcible removal of Indigenous children was a part of assimilation policies adopted by all Australian governments throughout the twentieth century.

One of the Report's recommendations was a national apology. Such an apology was given by the Rudd Labor Government in 2008, called the 'Sorry' speech.

The enquiry which produced the report spoke with a large number of Aboriginals, but it appears that it did not pay much attention to any other people affected by the report. The formal report tabled in parliament of the inquiry into the so-called stolen generation reached damning conclusions which were almost certainly unsound and relied on false claims and exaggerated complaints.

Was there a stolen generation?

On the issue of the 'stolen generation', Professor Keith Windschuttle in his voluminous accounts has stated that there never was a stolen generation as such. In other words, there was never a government policy of removing children from their natural parents or parent for the purpose of 'breeding out the colour' or of forcing them to develop in a non-Aboriginal environment. The Aboriginal descendants in Tasmania burnt Professor Windschuttle's books, but that action has no impact on what the books disclose. Recently, Professor Windschuttle has continued to state that the idea of the stolen generation is a myth.

The idea of forced removal as part of a strategy for forced assimilation may have been in reality merely imaginative analysis, although it is possible that some of the officials dealing with problems affecting Aboriginals held the views that they were sometimes believing that they were doing something to ameliorate problems by creating pressure on mothers to surrender their children because their home environments were hopelessly inadequate.

Cubillo and Gunner

Two of the few legal cases about children being taken from their homes that provide considerable detail and analysis of the subject are *Cubillo and Gunner v The Commonwealth*. The plaintiffs were chosen by advocates who considered Lorna Cubillo and Peter Gunner were good examples of Aboriginal children having been forcibly removed from their homes for reasons based upon racist views. Writs issued by or for 2000 indigenous people were pending in the Federal Court since 1996. Much depended on the outcome of these two cases.

On 11 August 2001, the judge handed down his reserved judgement in *Cubillo v Commonwealth* (2000). He rejected all the applicants' claims against the Commonwealth, while acknowledging the continuing trauma and suffering that resulted from their removal and detention.

The judge, Justice O'Loughlin of the Northern Territory Registry in Darwin held that 'at the relevant times, there was no general policy in force in the Northern Territory supporting the indiscriminate removal and detention of part-Aboriginal children, irrespective of the personal circumstances of each child'. The judgement delivered in this case runs for 700 pages. The judgement included the following significant passage:

> [Par. 28] The calibre of the former officers of the Native Affairs Branch and the Welfare Branch who gave evidence in this trial was exceptionally high. Many of them were highly educated and many subsequently achieved high postings in Government in later life. Their achievements are noted later in these reasons. My reason for mentioning this factor is to identify them as people of intelligence and experience who might be expected to have knowledge and awareness of the policies that existed in relation to Aboriginal and part-Aboriginal people and the manner in which those policies were implemented. As the summaries of their evidence will reveal, all of them denied the existence of a general or widespread policy of removal of part-Aboriginal children and most of them insisted that no child was removed without the consent of the mother of that child.

The activists were unable to make out a case for these chosen victims. The losers and their supporters simply rejected the conclusions of the presiding judge. The judgement was appealed against to the Full Court of the Federal Court, but the appeal was dismissed.

Other cases

Andrew Bolt, who, it is said, is the most widely read newspaper columnist in Australia, has written a number of articles in the *Herald-Sun* on the subject of the so-called 'stolen generation'. His position is that there were no stolen children. In February 2024, he had this to say:

> What a farce. On Tuesday – Sorry Day – Prime Minister Anthony Albanese declared his "proudest" day in politics was 16 years ago, when his mate Kevin Rudd said sorry to the "stolen generation". Yet in the next breath he announced that under him we'd taken more Aboriginal children than before.
>
> The numbers are incredible: more than 22,000 Aboriginal children are now in out of home care. They're 10 times more likely than other children to be removed from their parents to save them from being bashed, raped, starved or neglected ...
>
> Only a fool could believe such a smug and cartoonish story that officials who removed some Aboriginal children – 30, 40 or 50 years ago – were racist, cruel and genocidal, but the ones today who remove even more are just keeping them safe ...
>
> Please get your children and grandchildren to read this, too, to arm them against the lies.
>
> That's why our courts still haven't found even one case of a child stolen just for being Aboriginal.

Chapter Fourteen The stolen generation

The NSW Supreme Court ... ruled that an Aboriginal woman ... had not been stolen but ... given away by her mother.

Western Australia's Supreme Court ruled that seven children also weren't stolen but removed for their safety.

In Victoria, a Labor appointed stolen generation Taskforce could not find one truly stolen child and admitted the state had had "no formal policy for removing children" ...

... a Queensland appeal court heard a case involving an Aboriginal girl betrayed by the stolen generation myth. Three years earlier, when she was seven, she'd been raped in Aurukun in Cape York. She was found with syphilis and foetal alcohol syndrome. Eventually white foster parents in Cairns looked after her ... two social workers (required that she be sent back to Aurukun for a while). And there she was pack raped again – six times by nine men and boys. The court heard that rapists thought sex with a 10-year-old was normal ...

Who does this myth really help?

There appear to be few (if any) cases about the removal of full-blooded Aboriginals from their families. It is fair to say that a balanced view must be that part-Aboriginal children were often removed from their homes for good reasons involving their welfare, often from dysfunctional home environments or from situations where their partial non-Aboriginality invited discrimination from other members of the tribe as a result. We know, of course, that in remote communities in modern times, it is still the case that Aboriginal families often produce dysfunctional family environments to a much greater degree than comparable families outside those communities in the cities and towns (including Aboriginal families in those towns and cities).

Continuing issues

The Australian Domestic and Family Violence Clearinghouse (a respected national body whose board members are all at least part-Aboriginal) states that, based on offences reported to police in Western Australia, indigenous women are forty-five times more likely to experience family violence than non-Indigenous women and according to the government's Australian Institute of Health and Welfare, Indigenous people were thirty-two times more likely to be hospitalised for family violence as non-Indigenous people in 2016–2017.

The Australian Institute of Criminology published figures in January 2020 which indicated that in 2016–2017, about twenty-three per cent of intimate partner homicide victims were Indigenous people.

Fear of removal

The conclusion that there was no general policy of removing Aboriginal children from their home environment, and thus creating the stolen generation as such, does not amount to a denial of the experience of Aboriginal children growing up in earlier generations having a genuine fear of being removed from their families by government representatives. This attitude is recorded by Warren Mundine in his autobiography which indicates that it was real enough.

Where to now?

It is clear that legislation discriminated against Aboriginals in all States through welfare boards and controls. Warren Mundine discusses these issues in his autobiography and his account sounds quite credible. Happily, all such restrictions have gone. To be fair, the laws were generally meant to assist Aboriginals, not to persecute them. There have been many instances of legislation being passed by State governments before federation with the object of making special provision to support Aboriginals.

As the Australian government has formally apologised for the 'stolen generation' and as the concept has been accepted by many if not most people, it is difficult to conduct a fight back against the consensus which is typically supported by those wearing their guilt publicly for supposed sins of others, most of whom have passed on and are unavailable for useful contribution. However, the truth should be told and promulgated.

Chapter Fifteen

The compensation

Expenditure

The Productivity Commission estimated that government expenditure *per person* in 2012-2013 was $43,449 for Aboriginal and Torres Strait Islander Australians, compared with $20,900 for other Australians – a ratio of 2.08 to 1, an increase from the ratio of 1.93 to 1 in 2008-2009.

A 2014 report states that total direct expenditure on services for Aboriginal and Torres Strait Australians in 2012-2013 was estimated to be $30.3 billion, accounting for six point one per cent of total direct general government expenditure.

These figures are an important statement of what Australians at large pay for the descendants of the original inhabitants. Of course, it has been suggested that the $30 billion dollar figure includes a lot of welfare which would be available for other people and the direct expenditure on Aboriginals is 'only' about $6 billion dollars. The figures on expenditure per person tell a different story.

We do not know if the figures include the cost of having such a much larger percentage of Aboriginals kept in prisons. We also should know whether the costs of medical treatment are considered when the statistics indicate that Aboriginal women are thirty-five times more likely than other Australians to be hospitalised for domestic violence.

The total amount spent by state and federal governments and other institutions and agencies will probably never be known, but it is worthy of reflection.

Native title

According to Professor Keith Windschuttle, the amount of area now subject to native title is fifty-five per cent (and rising) of the total land area of Australia. Also, the additional area subject to proposed claims, if granted, will take the whole of the native title area to some sixty per cent of Australia, including about eighty per cent of Western Australia. It is worthy of note that there are about 40,000 Aboriginals living outside Perth in WA. The area affected by native title in Western Australia alone is as big as the whole of Western Europe, the home of hundreds of millions of people.

Professor Blainey in an article in *The Australian* in July 2023 wrote: 'Few Australian voters know of this fact. It constituted the largest transfer of land in the history of the modern world.'

Of course, quite a bit of the land subject to native title, particularly in Western Australia, would be of low value relative to a lot of land in Australia, but it is still a very large area.

While this form of title does not (at least, not yet) give the freehold of the land, it does, for example, mean that mining among other activities cannot be undertaken without the consent and profit sharing of the holders of native title.

It also means that others may be excluded from important

sites by the native title holders in many cases without any reasonable justification or, as in the case a few decades ago of the 'secret women's business' in South Australia, based on false and fraudulent claims.

It is fair to say that, apart from potential for mining, some if not a significant part of the area subject to native title applications and grants would be unsuitable for any useful agricultural pursuit or other developments. Nonetheless, there is undoubtedly considerable value in the land in aggregate.

Protection

As has been mentioned, the Aboriginals may have been fortunate in their choice of oppressors, as the British were rather more enlightened than many of their competing nations. In addition, the Aboriginals profited, probably more than most of us, from the victories in the wars that have been fought to protect all Australians.

We have discussed earlier in Part 2 the sacrifices made by our men and women and that these sacrifices made an important contribution to the success of the Allies in those conflicts. Our troops made a major contribution to prevent occupation of Australia by powers that, given their previous behaviour, would not have had any particular reason to hold our Aboriginal population in high regard.

Concessions

Other concessions have been available for Aboriginals for long periods of time. They include preferential treatment in work placement, special rates of taxes applicable to royalties received, availability of educational advantages of various types, housing loans not available to others and numerous other benefits provided by the community at large.

When this author was a young partner in a legal firm many, many years ago, the firm acted for the then Victorian Ministry for Aboriginal Affairs in conducting conveyancing transactions for persons of Aboriginal descent to acquire houses with a government grant of $1500, which at that time was sufficient to secure a loan for the balance of the price of a house with generally a bit left over. The ministry also paid the legal costs of the applicant so the services were provided at no charge to them. The firm had a good relationship with the buyers, as clients who do not have to pay fees are generally comfortable with one's work for them.

Summary

It will be seen that being an Aboriginal or part-Aboriginal in Australia has many advantages. One might have thought that the advantages might be subjected to a calculation providing a reduced amount of value if a person is only one-eighth or one-sixteenth of Aboriginal descent, but generally it will make no difference. Even a one-thirty-second may qualify ...

This is one of the reasons why the number of Aboriginals in Australia is increasing quite rapidly. Who would be silly enough to deny an Aboriginal ancestor? Of course, some people claiming Aboriginality may not have such ancestry. That would seem to be the likely case for Bruce Pascoe who, journalist Andrew Bolt complains, is unable to produce any documentary evidence of his claimed ancestry.

In total, we really have no idea what has been spent by Australians in general on benefits for Aboriginals. We have allocated, and are continuing to allocate, vast areas of land for their benefit. We have paid, and continue to pay, large and clearly disproportionate sums of money for the benefit of their current day descendants, including many partial descendants. We endow scholarships and whole university departments. We privilege them with employment and educational opportunities.

As mentioned more than once, many of our people made the ultimate sacrifice for those left behind after conflicts. In addition to the deaths in the wars, there were, of course, many more thousands who returned injured and impaired and often died soon afterwards.

We do find frequently that Australians are accused of being racist in some context or other. That suggests that the party making the criticism has never travelled. This author has never been in a country in which the members of the community at large have a better mindset towards people of different races than Australia. One might qualify that view by reflecting upon the absurd position of a relatively small number of anti-Semites who are busily protesting against the existence of the democratic State of Israel after the murderous onslaught of the terrorist group on 7 October 2023 in which over 1300 Israelis were murdered, raped or violently taken as hostages.

This author lived in England for two years and has seen racist conduct in the streets of London. He has also been to America

Chapter Fifteen The compensation

several times where racism is quite common. People are not old enough to recall that during World War II, the black American soldiers were amazed at the fact that they could travel around Melbourne on trams in which they were not segregated, even though we had the White Australia Policy.

Google states that in the United States, interracial marriages were forbidden in thirty-one states as late as 1960. In 1967, a Supreme Court ruling removed this restriction.

Racial prejudice abounds in Asia. In Thailand, recently, this author stayed at a block of beach apartments in which the compendium offered to guests sets out names of foreign racial groups whose members of which may not take an apartment in that building.

In addition to our lack of proclivity towards racism, we live in a society which in general is patently tolerant of people of differing backgrounds, politics, cultures, sexual inclinations, religions and those of no religion. When one reflects upon the mindset of people in countries such as the Muslim-majority countries, we know how the human condition there is subject to oppressions of which we are conspicuously free.

The obvious fact of large numbers of inter-racial marriages obviously gives the lie to the assertion that Australia is a racist country.

We should be proud of what has been done to help Aboriginals and compare how we have dealt with these complex issues with the conduct in other countries. In the United States, for example, there have been numerous treaties by governments with the native people, and it would seem that almost invariably the treaties are breached. In Brazil, the native people who have survived are in constant conflict with government.

We do not know when we will have expiated our sins and our guilt and that of our forebears, and it may well be time to assess the cost of that expiation to date and perhaps try to close the door on the past.

Of course, the issues of the relative poverty and social dysfunction of some Aboriginals is in one sense not connected to entitlements as a result of dispossession of land. It is a reflection of needs and poor choices, such as not ensuring that children attend school, and also indulging excessively in alcohol or drugs.

Recently, an activist complained that the appalling behaviour of many Aboriginal men towards their women (in particular in the tribal areas) was a result of British settlement. That seems rather a ludicrous stretch of the imagination. We know from accounts such as those of Watkin Tench, William Buckley, AJ Boyd and others that brutality of men towards women in Aboriginal society was the order of the day. Aboriginal women have gained a great deal from colonisation.

This author is totally opposed to a constitutional recognition for Aboriginal rights which would be contrary to all well-known charters of human rights and the fundamental democratic principle of equality of all before the law. This opposition has nothing to do with race. In addition, a change to effect such discrimination might continue indefinitely into the future, and we should not expect that the Aboriginals could possibly be given any more under a treaty than they have already received or are receiving.

Chapter Fifteen The compensation

With experiences of travelling in over sixty countries, this author is very happy to call Australia home, knowing that it is, even with its failings, the best place on earth to live. We should be very proud of our heritage and all of us, including the Aboriginals, should be grateful for those who have gone before us and brought us to this enlightened and welcoming country.

Professor Biggar, who has been quoted in Chapter Seven, had this to say about the position of natives:

> ... today's descendants of the Aboriginal people of the early nineteenth century - even [those] that languish in remote communities - now have the privilege of living in one of the most prosperous and liberal countries on earth.

Part Five
Moral issues and other issues

Chapter Sixteen

The moral issues

Of course, there is an issue about dispossession which involved taking over land which was not regularly in use by those who occupied it, because mostly they were nomadic; in Tasmania and Victoria, if not over most of the country, the tribes moved up to forty times a year. The reason they moved was mainly because they had no knowledge of cultivation of the soil and had no domestic animals used for the supply of food. Aboriginals living near rivers such as the Murray tended to move less frequently, presumably because they had more available fish.

Once that knowledge was available to them, the tribes no longer needed to be moving, because food could be, and was made, available from sources other than hunting and gathering. (It must have been exciting to have seen your first fruit trees growing after planting and seeing sheep when first available with wool and meat.) To insist that their wanderings over the countryside gave them a right to keep all others out of those areas would be quite absurd and immoral, not merely inconvenient. It would have been quite reasonable to require that they should forego any claim to at least part of the land no longer required so others could use it. The areas involved are huge relative to the number of people involved. Consider what the preservation of such a right would involve: an Aboriginal might wake up and walk several kilometres every day just to see if anybody else had visited his domain. It would have been a nonsense, and it still would be.

Of course, they claimed a spiritual connection with the land, but if you only saw it once or twice a year, the connection could not have been that close except in relation to some special feature of the land.

Aboriginals clearly had some special skills both in hunting and gathering. They used their skills in mimicry and controlled movement and their skill with their weapons for ensnaring and killing animals, and their bushcraft allowed them to see and obtain food from plants about which the Europeans were quite ignorant. However, their horizons for obtaining food sources would have been enlarged dramatically over time.

In relation to the land, the Europeans can fairly say that the land taken was paid for with the blood of many thousands of dead and injured in international conflicts, a conspicuously big advantage for Aboriginal tribes who would have been subjected to unimaginable treatment had our armies been unsuccessful. The first thing to go would have been land rights. Consider what the Japanese would have thought about native title had they been in charge. We were, of course, to be part of their Greater East Asia Co-Prosperity Area.

There has been a vast amount of money spent on Aboriginal welfare which has been largely supplied by the rest of us. The Europeans managed to establish and develop a very large country with numerous advantages in such things as houses, buildings, schools, hospitals and very much more with plenty of available space and also brought with them numerous advantages shared with the natives in which they had been precluded from participating because of their primitive and remote lifestyle. Apart from the substantial contributions made by Australians in many areas of human activity, Australia has provided vast quantities of food, minerals and other produce for people in other countries. Serious education including the ability to read and write were supplied to Aboriginals with little or no cost to them.

Not the least of the compensatory benefits has been the establishment of native title. Over half this very large country has been appropriated away from Europeans and their descendants. The reader is invited to reflect upon what the attitude would have been of the soldiers, who fought and died or suffered serious injuries during the world wars, concerning the grant to the chosen few of this entitlement to land, the collective size of dozens of countries, many with large populations and crowded cities.

By way of illustration, consider just a sample of Asian neighbours:

- Cambodia: population, 16,943,826; size of land, 116,520 km^2
- Thailand: population, 71,885,799; size of land, 513,130 km^2
- Japan: population, 122,631,432; size of land, 377,073 km^2
- Vietnam: population, 98.19 million; size of land, 331,210 km^2
- Philippines: population, 115.6 million; size of land, 300,000 km^2
- Australia: population, 26,664,848; size of land, 7,668,000 km^2.

On any analysis, Aboriginals in Australia have been significantly advantaged over others, many of whom have made very substantial contributions to our country and its development as arguably the best country in the world in which to live.

An alternative approach might have been to grant all full-blooded Aboriginals a reasonable parcel of land outright and for part-Aboriginals a smaller grant.

As mentioned above and worthy of note is that Australian farmers are regularly contributing food to fifty countries and to millions of people. One might reasonably ask what the Aboriginals were contributing to others.

Chapter Seventeen
Current issues

Honouring the past

If you, our reader, feels guilty about treatment of Aboriginals by your forebears or by others who were not your forebears, please do not impose your guilt upon this author or the rest of us. Restrain yourself.

If you feel we should honour what is considered Aboriginal culture, you should be sure to read all the chapters in this little book. What consisted of Aboriginal 'culture' was appallingly warlike, violent, primitive, cannibalistic and profoundly misogynistic. In fact, the serious level of misogyny was probably much worse than the contemporary state of the dreadful persecution of women in many Arab and Muslim communities.

Clearly, the culture was primitive in that a number of features of very old cultures which emerged in some cases over thousands of years in many parts of the rest of the world never surfaced in Aboriginal Australia - such as literature, buildings, transport, astronomy, reading and writing, arithmetic, cultivation, architecture and many other areas of learning - until the First Fleet.

This author has always admired the work of Albert Namatjira. He was obviously a world class artist, but there are not a large number of such artists able to be acknowledged in Australia. The comparisons are unnecessary but bear in mind, for example, the work of artists in Italy over hundreds of years, including the great Leonardo, Michelangelo, Titian, Caravaggio, Cellini and Raphael among others. What a wealth of art exists from all corners of the globe before you project a list of Aboriginal artists who obviously did not paint on canvas until after the arrival of the First Fleet.

The idea of foisting the Aboriginal culture upon our children who would otherwise be ignorant is absurd. There are only a small number of full-blooded Aboriginals, perhaps as few as 2 people in every 1000 members of our community. While there is no reason not to respect them because of their minute number, after what has been done to date, we no longer owe them any more than we do to other minority groups.

As far as the mixed-race members of our community, if a person is only part-Aboriginal, one would know that there is another heritage to consider, if not more, and in many cases, it will provide a noticeably more attractive recent history than that of the Aboriginals.

It also may reflect a much greater contribution to our national heritage and welfare than that part of them which is Aboriginal. In saying that, this author has always believed that in the case of marriages between people of different racial or ethnic backgrounds, the best of both worlds often emerges in the offspring of such unions. In the case of this author, six of his twelve grandchildren are Eurasian and they exemplify this belief of his. In addition, the author's oldest grandson has married a young lady from the Philippines.

Consider the inter-racial marriages of the Aboriginals. Of nearly a million people of Aboriginal ancestry, over ninety-five per cent of them are descended from Europeans and it is from this racial mixture that some of the most outstanding Indigenous leaders have emerged.

Other countries and groups which have contributed to Australia in many ways include:

- the English with, among many things, their outstanding contributions to the legal and parliamentary institutions, to literature (with Shakespeare among many others), the theatre and medicines, including vaccines
- the Irish (generally but not always Catholic) who built a school and a church in every town in Australia
- the Anglicans and Scottish Presbyterians who also built churches and schools and made major contributions in banking and construction
- the Germans who helped develop our wine industry
- the Chinese who (even before the White Australia policy happily collapsed) gave us Chinese restaurants with their distinctive cuisine in many hundreds of locations throughout the country
- the Italians who also gave us numerous restaurants and distinctive foods, real coffee and the continuing features of the ancient Roman Empire in such matters as roads and bridges
- the Jews (currently reviled by some of our more recent

and less welcome migrants and their ignorant, obnoxious and juvenile supporters) who contributed, vastly in excess of their relative numbers, in numerous areas of activity, including our greatest soldier, Sir John Monash. When he died in 1931, a crowd estimated to be up to 300,000 people gathered in the streets of Melbourne for his state funeral procession when the total population of the city was 995,000. Their small numbers have also contributed massively to philanthropic causes of all faiths without any reservation about the characters of those enjoying their generosity. Our first Australian-born Governor-General was Sir Isaac Isaacs, who was Jewish.

- the Welsh who, with the people of Cornwall, helped to conduct one of the world's great copper mines
- the Greeks who made Melbourne one of the leading Greek cities in the world and incidentally gave us the great early philosophers
- the French who, as well as their cuisine, gave us some of the great works of literature and philosophy.

This is not intended by any means to be an exhaustive list, as people from many countries have made important contributions. When one considers countries such as India, Thailand and the Philippines that have recently had large population increases in their Australian populations, their people and cultures will surely enhance Australia's cultural heritage over time.

This list is also not designed to suggest that Aboriginal people have not contributed to Australia's welfare, but simply to highlight what other groups have done, and which have every right to feel that acknowledgement of these contributors should not be passed by because of a supposed need to celebrate so-called Aboriginal culture.

Welcome to country

The recently introduced so-called 'Welcome to country' is simply a way of giving offence to the current owners of the land. They did not steal the land, but they bought it often with great sacrifice and very hard work.

If one acknowledges that most Aboriginals generally travelled over large areas of land over time, it is a simple arrogance to suggest that they held, at any stage, rights to areas simply because they had traversed it during their nomadic days.

If it had been a practice for Aboriginals, it would be entirely appropriate to welcome visitors to a country in which the welcoming party lived or which he or she occupied. But what possible logic would have you welcome someone to a country in which you have no current interests, in which you do not live and which is owned by someone else who can reasonably object to your arrogance and offensiveness in attempting to deceive the visitors that you are in a position to allow them entry when you are doing so with someone else's rights? At best, this silly practice is patronising and offensive to people who have genuine respect for those who have gone before.

In one of the few reliable and extensive sources on the subject of Aboriginal practices, William Buckley does not appear to have witnessed very many occasions (if any) which could be described as a formal welcome to country. More often, a tribe would be creeping up on another tribe before murdering a few of their members.

In his autobiography, Buckley mentions by name a number of tribes, including the following: Pootmaro, Yaawangis, Bengali, Waarenghadawa, Putnaroo, Warawaroo, Watourongs. The last two were said to be generally at war with each other. In addition, Buckley mentions contact with quite a number of tribes which he had encountered without providing us with names. The number might be as many as another ten to fifteen. The numbers of 'welcome to country' he describes: nil. Tribes did come together and were not invariably hostile to each other and sometimes joined in corroborees. Conflict, however, was constant.

An article by Lincoln Brown in *The Spectator* of April 2022 included the following:

> White people, as nebulous as that concept is, are not guests in Australia. My ancestors were also born and raised here many generations ago. No one should be made to feel guilty for the colour of their skin or blamed for the actions of people who have long since died. This attribution of historical, collective guilt to an entire group of people due to their ethnicity is not only racist but is a symptom of a dying Australia. It is a direct, ideological assault on Western values based on selective distortions of history and the Marxist idea of class guilt, now applied to race, which divides humanity into 'oppressed' and 'oppressor' classes and ascribes sinfulness or virtue based on whatever group one happens to belong to.

Recently, the presenters of the Sky News program, 'The

Outsiders', have commenced a campaign to rid us of this odious practice. When asked to give a 'welcome' a few years ago, this author announced that we should honour the original founders of our city, John Pascoe Fawkner and John Batman.

Naming

Putting forward that we should be obliged to adopt place names from some supposed Aboriginal word in place of the use of the name of some famous non-Aboriginal person is preposterous and deeply offensive. Bear in mind that, almost without exception, almost all land, including the use of land, was obtained at some stage, however long ago, by conquest. To pretend otherwise is nonsense. Bear in mind also that for Australians, the majority of their roots still spring originally from England, Scotland and Ireland. While that does not preclude us from considering others, there is ample justification for naming places after some of our amazing ancestors rather than members of a tribe who were invariably deeply misogynistic, in many cases cannibalistic and generally warlike. Wake up!

There would still be room to adopt an Aboriginal name when it offered some feature of advantage. Originally Rose Hill, the name was changed to Parramatta which followed the Aboriginal word then in use, *burramatta*. The new name was not difficult to say nor to remember. Canberra also seems to have had an origin in an Aboriginal word.

Celebration of past leaders

The overwhelming majority of Aboriginals, in fact over ninety-five per cent, are descended from one or more ancestors who were not born in Australia. Among those ancestral personnel and their places of origin, there are obviously many that we can celebrate. We know there were many great men before us. Because a person thinks that celebrating someone else's ancestry is not celebrating their own provides no right to object to that other party's celebration.

Australia Day

As has been said, Australia Day was not the day the First Fleet arrived in Australia. It was the day when the flag was raised for the new settlement after an extraordinary voyage. It was the date agreed upon by all Australian governments to be a date for celebration.

The distinguished writer, Professor Henry Ergas, writing in his column for *The Australian* in January 2022 had this to say:

It is ... an illusion to expect any event of historical significance to be viewed through a prism of unanimity and the more significant it is, the less likely it is to be universally hailed ...

Ultimately, that is why patriotism matters, and especially so in democracies, because nations provide the constitutional framework, and the symbolic glue, that defines our identification with, our responsibility for, and our allegiance to, a community that reaches far beyond our private affairs. Never perfect but always striving, our country is the home we inherit, with its ghosts but also its joys and comforts and the scope to renovate, extend and improve. If Australia Day reminds us of that, it will have more than earned its keep.

The Uluru Statement from the Heart

In a lengthy article in *The Australian*, 1–2 July 2023, Professor Blainey criticises the Uluru Statement from the Heart, including the following comments:

> [It] is a vulnerable document. If it is sometimes silent when Aboriginal families are visible, but vocal in condemning Australian people for misdeeds that never happened ... The ancestors of most mainstream Australians painfully lost their lands in some faraway era and received no compensation ... ancient Aboriginal people themselves were champions at dispossessing their neighbours ... in every known part of the world the semi-nomadic hunters and gatherers had been deadly in their tribal warfare ...
>
> ... Parliament in its recent debate did nothing to validate the Uluru accusation that mainstream Australians had refused for generations even to count Aboriginal people ...

The Commonwealth officers conducting the first federal census in 1911 were instructed to count full-blooded Aboriginals. It may be assumed that part-Aboriginals would have been counted without the necessity for specifying them. (Of course, they were also part-European).

Professor Blainey goes on:

> ... Understandably, the officers had to retreat when they reached remote areas where local inhabitants had seen no white person nor heard a word of English. But tens of

thousands of Aboriginal people were counted often with enormous effort in the accessible regions ...

... South Australia, holding a census on Sunday April 2, 1871, recorded the exact districts and towns where more than 5000 Aboriginal men and women lived ... On the same day in gold-rich Victoria ... all races were counted ... in the late 1850s, in the three populous Australian colonies, most Aboriginal men were allowed to vote.

The Uluru Statement claims, among other things, that there is a remaining sovereignty held by Aboriginals which lives alongside the rights of the Crown. It also claims that their young are in prison and implies that they should not be. It asks for something like a truth telling commission and would suggest that Aboriginals should conduct it. What is being sought is a review of the plight of Aboriginals in Australia without the involvement of any other Australians, being most of the members of the community. Our prime minister claims to support this peculiar position.

The trouble with truth telling is that it would need to be honest. The present indications are that it would never be honest as its grand mission is based on falsehoods. Are the Aboriginals in prison for something they did not do? Alternatively, are their disproportionate numbers in incarceration a reflection of the totally disproportionate number of their women who have had to be hospitalised for domestic violence caused by their menfolk or their totally disproportionate numbers of homicides pointed out by Senator Price in her speech (referred to in Chapter 8 of this book)?

To be honest would mean to have a serious look at the history of misogyny, domestic violence, cannibalism, infanticide, paedophilia and tribal warfare, all of which have been standout areas of activity for the native population before the First Fleet arrived. Sadly, some of these customary activities still survive among some Aboriginals.

The Australian published an article by Mirko Bagaric, an academic lawyer, in January 2020 which includes the following:

> One in fifty indigenous people is in prison ... they are the most disadvantaged people in our community ... The mass incarceration of indigenous Australians is the most serious human rights crisis of our nation and our time. ...
>
> The best approach to reducing the unfair and discriminatory burden that our criminal justice system inflicts on indigenous Australians [who are about twice as likely to be imprisoned even for the same offence as non-indigenous offenders] is to provide a concrete mathematical sentencing discount for such offenders [and the] discount that is appropriate is 25 per cent.

This is certainly a most unusual suggestion for dealing with the issues. This author would like to know the source of the claim that Indigenous offenders are twice as likely to be imprisoned for the same offence as non-Indigenous. On the surface, it would seem to be highly improbable. Does it take into account, for instance, the repeat offending which obviously affects sentencing? The Royal Commission proposed by Senator Price, and rejected by the Australian Labor Party Government, would have been a suitable vehicle to enquire about this claim.

A reasonable question is whether the best part of 20,000 Indigenous are in prison as claimed, being one in fifty of all Indigenous.

Wikipedia claims:

- As of 30 June 2021, preliminary Australian Bureau of Statistics' estimates indicate that 984,000 First Nations people were living in Australia, representing three point eight per cent of the total Australian population. [One in every fifty would be 19,680.]
- Aboriginal and Torres Strait Islander prisoners accounted for thirty-three per cent of all prisoners.
- Ninety-one per cent (12,540) of Aboriginal and Torres Strait Islander prisoners were male, nine per cent (1309) were female.
- The median age was 33.2 years.
- Eighty per cent (10,828) had experienced prior adult imprisonment.

Obviously the two sources cannot both be accurate.

Another article in *The Australian* in January 2020 approaches the issues from a different angle. The author was Nicola Berkovic, and her article includes the following:

Australian Institute of Criminology research manager Samantha Bricknell said figures involving Aboriginal and Torres Strait Islander victims *stand out* because of over-representation and because such a high proportion were perpetrated by family members, when compared with the non-indigenous population ...

Gary Bentley has been fighting for changes to the way

police and other services respond to Aboriginal survivors of abuse since his sister Andrea Pickett was murdered by her estranged husband 10 years ago.

Australia's National Research Organisation for Women's Safety chief executive Heather Nancarrow said the "very significant over-representation of indigenous people, who make up less than 3% of the population, pointed to the limitations of mainstream responses to family violence for those communities ..."

Antoinette Braybrook, who heads a peak body representing indigenous survivors of abuse, said a dedicated national action plan to reduce violence against indigenous women and children was needed ... "when it comes to Aboriginal and Torres Strait Islander women we've got a national emergency, a national crisis on our hands ..."

... there has been anger over a recent decision to scrap funding for the body Ms. Braybrook heads ...

Ms. Braybrook said money earmarked to reduce violence against Aboriginal women and children was insufficient ...

Looking from a distance, one gets the impression that the one thing the ALP Federal Government does not do is listen to the women. It probably responds more favourably to a male academic lawyer who, it would seem, is more interested in protecting the perpetrators of crime rather than the victims.

John Tippett QC, a leading Northern Territory criminal barrister, is reported as saying: 'Men who beat Aboriginal women do not face disapproval in their own communities. They are not stripped of their positions on the local council for beating their wife ... It's not culturally part of a taboo.' He also says that children in families where these men live are living in a toxic environment.

Some Aboriginal offenders spend most of their adult lives in prison. When released, they return to their former criminal activities.

The Aboriginal flag

The Australian Aboriginal flag was designed by Aboriginal artist Harold Thomas in 1971, and it was first flown in Adelaide in July of that year. Thomas held the intellectual property rights to the flag's design until January 2022 when he transferred the copyright to the Commonwealth government. Apparently, a payment of $20 million dollars was made for the copyright of the flag.

Why did the Aboriginals need a flag? Before the First Fleet arrived, Aboriginals would probably never have seen a flag of any sort. Who decided that there should be a flag? Did we have a voice in how much might be spent on a flag for Aboriginals? It seems quite extraordinary if we have paid this huge amount of money for some sort of weird tokenism.

One can imagine that, if it was thought appropriate to have such a flag, a competition might have been conducted with a prize of, say, up to $100,000 for the selected artistry. There would most likely have been hundreds of submissions from which to choose.

In fact, it is entirely inappropriate to have one Aboriginal flag, as the Aboriginals were not a single group but consisted of hundreds of tribes which were as likely to have been fighting with other tribes than celebrating with a flag for all of them.

This expenditure on this item was totally beyond being reasonable if it had any justification at all. As for flying the flag in company with our national flag, it is simply a profound insult to our community. As many countries have been original contributors to those Australians who have been descendants from their citizens, should we not produce flags for various countries of origin of groups who, in many cases, number many more than the descendants of Aboriginals? The reality is that we need only one national flag, and that is the flag of the nation to which we belong.

Chapter Eighteen

The gap

Quoting again from the economist, Professor Henry Ergas, when writing for *The Australian* on 20 June 2020, had this to say:

> The indigenous Australians account for 30% of (Australia's) prisoners ... by the time they reach the age of 23, 75% of young indigenous people in NSW will have been cautioned by police, referred to a youth justice conference or convicted of an offence ... compared with 17% of their non-indigenous counterparts.
>
> ... (from 2015 to 2020) nearly a quarter of the indigenous male population has been arrested and more than 10% jailed ...
>
> ... the fault does not lie in the criminal justice system ... they are disproportionately represented in ... jails ... because they are far more likely to commit violent offences.

He goes on to quote from a most eminent criminologist that: the overwhelming weight of evidence confirms that differences in rates of offending (and reoffending) account for most, if not all, of the difference in imprisonment rates ... And it was not indigenous Australians who removed the prohibitions on the consumption of alcohol by, and the sale of alcohol to, Aboriginal people that had been in force throughout Australia since 1929 ...

... demeaning the past does nothing to heal the present ...

... the unstated premise that has led to the present calamity: that indigenous Australians are essentially a separate race, who should be funded to live at enormous expense in places where there are no viable jobs, where supplying basic services is prohibitively expensive and where alcohol and drugs are the only antidote to squalor, boredom and despair.

In the same year and in a different edition of the same newspaper, *The Australian*'s Indigenous Affairs correspondent reported that:

... the Australian Institute of Health and Welfare [released data showing] 57% of people aged between 10-17 in detention were Aboriginal and Torres Strait Islanders ... despite Indigenous Australians making up just 6% of the population of that age.

The situation with Aboriginals nowadays is that the vast majority of people of Aboriginal ancestry also have ancestry from other ethnic groups. The major problem areas seem to be when there has been little intermingling of ethnic backgrounds. Although being as ignorant as most people, this author believes that the excessive incidence of poor behaviour and low levels of assimilation with other groups comes from those Aboriginal communities where traditional tribal culture has a serious influence. That has to be an explanation for the huge difference between Indigenous and non-Indigenous rates of incarceration for domestic violence offences including violent assaults and murders, and the huge numbers of hospitalisations of women injured in such occurrences compared with the numbers for other groups.

One constant seems to be a lack of education in remote communities. There is also a lack of involvement in regular employment which makes available time to be spent cultivating vices such as over-indulgence in alcohol and drugs.

One critical historical conflict of ideas was reflected in the work of Geoffrey Partington in his book, *Hasluck versus Coombs: White Politics and Australia's Aborigines*. Professor Partington wrote as follows:

> If asked ... the overwhelming majority of the Australian people as a whole, and very likely a majority of Aborigines, would agree with Hasluck that the future of Aborigines ought not to be a matter for Aborigines alone to determine, any more than it would be the right to exclude Aborigines from participating in the determination of the future of non-Aboriginal Australians. It is ironical that ... we should find such an emphasis on the exclusive right of self-determination of a minority group, or rather of a set of related minority groups, most of whose members live intermingled with non-members. The real challenge that faces us all is to ensure that the living standards and opportunities in life of Aborigines should be broadly comparable to those of non-Aborigines, while at the same time respecting that some Aborigines may wish to exercise different choices from those made by most other Australians. Different choices lead

to different outcomes, some of which may be unpleasant but that is the nature of choice.

Marcia Langton, a prominent indigenous academic, attacked Partington in particular by defaming him about his footnotes as being 'shonky', which in fact they were clearly not as became obvious after lengthy analysis by Professor Blainey.

Marcia Langton can join Linda Burney and the Uluru Statement in stating as facts things that were simply not true in relation to Indigenous and to non-Aboriginal Australians. They do no credit to their cause if they wish to help other Aboriginals by being flippant with the truth, whether deliberate or not. It is the same sort of flippancy which allows Bruce Pascoe to dissemble apparently with impunity.

One might ask Linda Burney and Marcia Langton what their real agenda is. If they can offer non-facts to support their cause and take not the slightest trouble to check their facts against available sources, why should they be taken seriously? Any official or academic who offers support to Bruce Pascoe and his fantasies should lose their job.

While it would be pretentious to think that there is a solution which has avoided governments for many years, this author would like to make some suggestions which may not be novel.

Warren Mundine, in his very well-presented autobiography, considers that the essential need for people in poverty or who are welfare dependent is economic participation. In this regard, it is interesting to recall a famous quotation of John Maynard Keynes, as follows:

If the Treasury were to fill old bottles with banknotes, bury them at suitable depths in disused coal mines which are then filled up to the surface with town rubbish, and leave it to private enterprise on well-tried principles of laissez-faire, to dig the notes up again ... there need be no more unemployment, and, with the help of the repercussions, the real income of the community, and its capital wealth also, would probably become a good deal more than it actually is.

Some years ago, this author wrote a book on taxation and welfare reform in which it was proposed that we should consider seriously the introduction of a universal basic income with some qualifications. The idea was not that anyone should receive income for nothing. On the contrary, in this scheme with some exceptions, you would be required to contribute, unless you were physically disabled, by working for at least twenty hours per week in any job you could get, or if not, you had to volunteer for working at least fifteen hours per week in any role allocated to you by government in charitable or other activities. If you did not comply, you earned nothing.

Consideration of a universal basic income may have an interesting new supporter in Professor Geoffrey Hinton. He is a computer scientist regarded as the 'godfather of AI'. He is the pioneer of neural networks, which form the theoretical basis of the current explosion in artificial intelligence. Until last year, he worked for Google. He is reported as having said, 'I was consulted by people in Downing Street, and I advised them that universal basic income was a good idea.'

While it may be premature to be considering a general

Chapter Eighteen The gap

universal basic income, the idea could well be used in remote communities to ensure that nobody would be entitled to receive any government support for their ordinary maintenance unless they made some sort of serious contribution to the community.

The idea of 'sit down money' should be removed completely. If it is suggested that there may be no work, available reference may be had to the quote of John Maynard Keynes if necessary, and work can be manufactured. That would seem to be the vague plan of the present ALP Government in relation to production of 'green' products, including energy.

Finally, it is imperative that government employees should supervise and administer the distribution of any funds in a community where this evil conduct, being either the bullying and intimidation of women and children on the one hand or the use of drugs and excessive alcohol on the other hand, is occurring. Equally, if children do not attend school, then their parents must lose their entitlement to government funding. If people in such a community can demonstrate that they have no culpability in these practices, then they would no longer be subject to government supervision. It is obviously pointless to continue the 'same old, same old' treatment of abuses of the system. What is done at the moment does not work.

In *The Australian*, 30 September 2024, an independent historian, Andrew McDermott, wrote as follows:

> Indigenous policy has been our greatest failure … In society where all Australians depend upon each other – economically, socially, politically – the notion that any group can be "self-determined" is a fantasy. Fifty years after a

Whitlam government raised the fantasy into a religion, it's time reality was given a stronger say.

As far as our federal government is concerned, they have rejected the proposal to have a Royal Commission into the abuses towards women and children in remote communities. Instead, they bleat on about the absurd notion of treaties and other nonsense. With whom do they wish to make treaties? A tribe with twenty or thirty people? A group of people who are part-Aboriginal and part-Irish? Between 150 and 250 treaties in different languages for all the known tribes? Thousands of people would be rejecting their European ancestry in favour of an ancestry which was quite frequently misogynistic, warlike, abusive of children, cannibalistic, illiterate and polygamous and which practised infanticide, endorsed child marriages of young girls with older men and the spearing of wives in the thigh if they were disagreeable. Of course, one can say that the other ancestors from other traditions were not babes in the woods, but they also provided some very positive and beneficial cultural traditions, many of which in general are more worthy of celebrating.

Part of that nonsense was to encourage municipal councils to cease conducting ceremonies of citizenship on Australia Day, which is a disgraceful and pathetic rejection and in total disregard of mainstream Australia.

Bibliography

Blainey, Geoffrey, *The Triumph of the Nomads: A History of Ancient Australia*, (Sun Books, Melbourne, 1985), *The Tyranny of Distance*, (Pan Macmillan, Australia, 2001).

Boyd, AJ, *Old Colonials*, (Gordon & Gotch, London, 1882)

Bradley, Phillip, *Hell's Battlefield: to Kokoda and beyond*, (Allen & Unwin, Sydney, 2013)

Brodie, Nick, *1787: The Lost Chapters of Australia's Beginnings*, (Hardie Grant Books, Sydney, 2016)

Buckley, William, (ed. Tim Flannery), *The Life and Adventures of William Buckley*, (Text Classics, Melbourne, 2017)

Campbell, Judy, *Invisible Invader: Smallpox and other diseases in Aboriginal Australia 1780-1880*, (MUP, Melbourne. 2002)

Crittenden, Victor, *The Voyage of the First Fleet*, (Mulini Press, Canberra, 1981)

de Moore, Greg, *Tom Wills, First Wild Man of Australian Sport*, (Allen & Unwin, Sydney, 2023)

Duffy, James P, *War at the End of the World: Douglas MacArthur and the Forgotten Fight for New Guinea, 1942-1945*, (Dutton Caliber, US, 2016)

Ferrante et al., 'Measuring the extent of domestic violence', (https://research-repository.uwa.edu.au/en/publications/measuring-the-extent-of-domestic-violence, The University of Western Australia, 1996)

Frost, Alan, *The First Fleet: The Real Story*, (Black Inc., Melbourne, 2012), *Botany Bay and the First Fleet*, (Black Inc., Melbourne, 2019)

Georgetown Institute for Women, Peace and Security and Peace Research Institute Oslo, 'Women, Peace, and Security Index 2023/24: Tracking sustainable peace through inclusion, justice, and security for women', (Washington, DC: GIWPS and PRIO, 2023)

Harris, John W, *One Blood: 200 years of Aboriginal encounter with Christianity: a story of hope*, (Albatross Books, Sutherland NSW, 1994)

Hughes, Robert, *The Fatal Shore*, (Collins Harvill, London, 1987)

Keeley, Lawrence H, *War Before Civilization: The Myth of the Peaceful Savage*, OUP (US), New York, 1998

Keynes, John Maynard, *The General Theory of Employment, Interest, and Money*, (Palgrave Macmillan, UK, 1936)

Moore, John, *The First Fleet Marines, 1786-1792*, (University of Queensland Press, Brisbane, 1987)

O'Brien, Peter, *Bitter Harvest: The illusion of Aboriginal Agriculture in Bruce Pascoe's Dark Emu*, (Quadrant Books, Australia, 2019)

Partington, Geoffrey, *Hasluck versus Coombs: White Politics and Australia's Aborigines*, (Quakers Hill, Sydney, Press, 1996)

Perry, Roland, *Monash and Chauvel*, (Allen & Unwin, Sydney, 2017)

Reynolds, Henry, *Why Weren't We Told?* (Penguin, Australia, 2000), *Forgotten War*, (UNSW, Sydney, 2013)

Tench, Watkin, (ed. Tim Flannery), *1788*, (Text Classics, Melbourne, 2012)

Viale, Charles R, 'Japan's Goals and Strategy in World War II', (Defence Technical Information Center, USA, https://apps.dtic.mil/sti/tr/pdf/ADA202272.pdf, 1988)

Walker, Frank, *Traitors*, (Hachette, Sydney, 2017)

Windschuttle, Keith, *The Fabrication of Aboriginal History, Vol. 1*, (Macleay Press, Paddington, NSW, 2002), *Vol. 3*, (Macleay Press, Paddington, NSW, 2009.)

www.ingramcontent.com/pod-product-compliance
Lightning Source LLC
Chambersburg PA
CBHW030328080526
44584CB00012B/758